FOUNDATIONS
for Knowing
God

1st Edition

ISBN 978-0-9997895-8-2

Contents

GOD

What God is Like

The Father's Desire for Relationship

WHAT GOD IS LIKE

HIS LOVING NATURE

God is love. (1 John 4:16)

The Bible does not say God "is loving." It says God is love. What is the difference?

_____

_____

Can you imagine what it would be like to know someone who was completely loving all the time? Describe what it would be like.

_____

_____

Is God's love altogether different from theirs? (Where does their lovingkindness come from?)

_____

_____

What Love Looks Like

There was a man who had two sons. The younger one said to his father, "Father, give me my share of the estate." So he divided his property between them. Not long after that, the younger son got together all he had, set off for a distant country and there squandered his wealth in wild living. After he had spent everything, there was a severe famine in that whole country, and he began to be in need. So he went and hired himself out to a citizen of that country, who sent him to his fields to feed pigs. He longed to fill his stomach with the pods that the pigs were eating, but no one gave him anything.

When he came to his senses, he said, "How many of my father's hired men have food to spare, and here I am starving to death! I will set out and go back to my father and say to him: 'Father, I have sinned against heaven and against you. I am no longer worthy to be called your son; make me like one of your hired men.'" So he got up and went to his father.

But while he was still a long way off, his father saw him and was filled with compassion for him. He ran to his son, threw his arms around him and kissed him. The son said to him, "Father, I have sinned against heaven and against you. I am no longer worthy to be called your son." But the father said to his servants, "Quick! Bring the best robe and put it on him. Put a ring on his finger and sandals on his feet. Bring the fattened calf and kill it. Let's have a feast and celebrate. For this son of mine was dead and is alive again; he was lost and is found." So they began to celebrate. (Luke 15:11-24)

The father in this story represents God. The son represents those who are living selfishly. At first how did the son treat the Father?

_____

How did the father treat the son back? Was he mean at any time?

_____

When the son returned, did the father wait to see what the son's attitude was before he showed love to him?

_____

What does this say about the father's love for the son?

_____

Based on how the father responded when the son came back, how do you think the father felt while his son was far away, living the party life?

_____

Even though the father loved the son unconditionally, what step did the son have to take in order to restore the relationship?

_____

God will always love you even if are far away from Him, but what step do we take in order to relate to Him and feel His love back?

_____

God's kindness leads you toward repentance. (Romans 2:4)

Does God use cruel punishments or threats to make you love Him? What does He use instead?

_____

8

What is the result of allowing God's love into your life?

_____

Why do you think God wants you to repent? How does this show He loves you?

_____

_____

Loving Completely

For God so loved the world that He gave His one and only Son, that whoever believes in Him shall not perish but have everlasting life. For God did not send his Son into the world to condemn the world but to save the world through Him. (John 3:16-17)

What was God's motivation to send Jesus to die for you?

_____

Does God want to send people to hell? How can you tell?

_____

_____

When we were still God's enemies, we were reconciled to Him through the death of his Son (Romans 5:10).

Did Jesus die for you because you were good enough?

_____

_____

Imagine someone who hates you. Now imagine a person whom you love with your whole heart. Can you imagine sending the one whom you love, to die? Would you send them to die in order to save the life of the one who hates you? What does this say about the kind of love God has for you?

_____

_____

You have heard that it was said, 'Love your neighbor and hate your enemy.' But I tell you: Love your enemies and pray for those who persecute you, that you may be sons of your Father in heaven. He causes his sun to rise on the evil and the good, and sends rain on the righteous and the unrighteous. If you love those who love you, what reward will you get?... Your Heavenly Father is perfect. (Matthew 5:43-48)

Does God only love those who love Him?

_____

What is God's attitude toward those who curse Him?

_____

_____

Is this just a metaphor, or does He actually do nice things for them? What two examples does Jesus give?

_____

_____

These are just general examples. Can you imagine other practical ways that God shows love or blesses those who hate Him?

_____

_____

Regardless of whether you have loved him or hated Him, what is God's attitude toward you?

_____

Have you ever done anything deeply wrong? According to this passage, what was God's attitude toward you while you were doing it?

_____

_____

Love is patient. Love is kind. It does not envy, it does not boast, it is not proud. It is not rude. It is not self-seeking. It is not easily angered. It keeps no record of wrongs. Love does not delight in evil but rejoices with the truth. It always protects, always trusts, always hopes, always perseveres. Love never fails. (1 Corinthians 13:4-8)

This is how the Bible defines love. Since God loves you, describe what His attitude is toward you.

_____

_____

Is God patient with you when you make a mistake?

_____

When you are rude or selfish, how does God respond to you in return?

_____

Does God protect you?

_____

Does God trust you?

_____

Based on this description of His love, what kind of personality do you think Jesus has? What is He like?

_____

_____

Does this description of Jesus differ from anything you have believed about Him in the past? If so, how?

_____

_____

Loving Him and Others Well

We love because He first loved us. (1 John 4:19)

What do you have to receive in your heart before you can truly love God or others?

_____

As the Father has loved me, so have I loved you. Now remain in my love. (John 15:9)

Is it just Jesus who loves you? Where did Jesus' love for you come from?

_____

What is supposed to be the effect of receiving God's love?

_____

What kinds of things come against you to fight "remaining" (or "abiding") in His love?

_____

_____

How could you combat those?

_____

_____

If you keep my commands, you will remain in my love, just as I have kept my Father's commands and remain in his love. I have told you this so that my joy may be in you and that your joy may be complete. My command is this: Love each other as I have loved you. Greater love has no one than this: to lay down one's life for one's friends. You are my friends if you do what I command.   (John 15:10-14)

If you obey Jesus' commands to love, where will you remain?

_____

If you obey His commands to love, how will you feel? How will Jesus feel?

_____

What is the sign that God loves you with *everything* He has?

_____

If you love God and others as sacrificially as Jesus desires, will you be taken care of? How will you get the love you need?

_____

_____

They asked Him, "Teacher, which is the greatest commandment in the Law?" Jesus replied: "'Love the Lord your God with all your heart and with all your soul and with all your mind.' This is the first and greatest commandment. And the second is like it: 'Love your neighbor as yourself.' All the Law and the Prophets hang on these two commandments." (Matthew 22:36-40)

There are many instructions in the Bible, but what does Jesus say is the goal of everything God wants?

_____

_____

When the Word tells you not to do something, how can love be God's motivation behind it?

_____

_____

→ God's love is the first thing we need to process as believers because it bonds us to Him. It causes us to walk with Him. We listen to Him, obey Him, stay with Him... because we love Him and we know He loves us.

→ He is Emmanuel, "God with us." His "with us" nature goes all the way through, in all of life.

HAVING A RECEPTIVE HEART

A farmer went out to sow his seed. As he was scattering the seed, some fell along the path, and the birds came and ate it up. Some fell on rocky places, where it did not have much soil. It sprang up quickly, because the soil was shallow. But when the sun came up, the plants were scorched, and they withered because they had no root. Other seed fell among thorns, which grew up and choked the plants. Still other seed fell on good soil, where it produced a crop – a hundred, sixty or thirty times what was sown. He who has ears, let him hear... (Matthew 13:3-9)

...Listen then to what the parable of the sower means: When anyone hears the message about the kingdom and does not understand it, the evil one comes and snatches away what was sown in his heart. This is the seed sown along the path. The one who received the seed that fell on rocky places is the man who hears the word and at once receives it with joy. But since he has no root, he lasts only a short time. When trouble or persecution comes because of the word, he quickly falls away. The one who received the seed that fell among the thorns is the man who hears the word, but the worries of this life and the deceitfulness of wealth choke it, making it unfruitful.

But the one who received the seed that fell on good soil is the man who hears the word and understands it. He produces a crop, yielding a hundred, sixty or thirty times what was sown. (Matthew 13:18-23)

Think about the process of growing a plant from a seed, to bearing fruit like an apple tree. How long does this take?

_____

What kind of steps are involved in cultivating a real plant long enough to bear fruit?

_____

_____

What kinds of obstacles does Jesus say a plant will face before it reaches maturity?

_____

_____

If the "seed" represents God's truth, and the "soil" represents your heart, what two things do you need to grow strong in God's Kingdom?

_____

_____

Based on this passage, is following God is supposed to be easy?

_____

_____

Who comes to distract you whenever you hear the truth? What does he do?

_____

_____

Some people hear the truth and start down the right path but give up following God. Why do they quit?

_____

_____

Some people keep the truth privately in their hearts, yet do not bear any fruit. Why not?

_____

_____

According to this passage, in order to survive and bear fruit, you must have deep roots. How can you prepare your own heart to have the roots go deep?

_____

_____

→ Receiving truth in our hearts does not mean "knowing" things intellectually or doctrinally. It isn't about thinking or mentally acknowledging true statements, or recognizing when others say them. It is about replacing what we believe with what God says, and letting those truths change us. We let them move through us, change us, and transform us to become a different person—to become like Him.

→ Love is the very first thing He wants to have change us.

REFLECTION QUESTION:

❖ Who is God? What is His nature?
   → *Can I believe this?*

THE FATHER'S DESIRE FOR RELATIONSHIP

CREATED FOR RELATIONSHIP

In the beginning was the Word, and the Word was with God, and the Word was God. He was with God in the beginning. Through Him all things were made; without Him nothing was made that has been made. In Him was life, and that life was the light of all mankind. (John 1:1-4)

When God the Father created the world, was he alone?

_____

Jesus said... "Father, glorify me in your presence with the glory I had with you before the world began." (John 17:5)

Who was with God before the world was created?

_____

What does it sound like their relationship was like?

_____

Then God said, "Let us make mankind in our image, in our likeness..." (Genesis 1:26)

Who does the "us" refer to when God created the world?

_____

Why do you think God wanted to create mankind? Does he want a relationship with you?

_____

_____

God exists in relationship, and he created mankind out of that relationship. If you are made in his image, what does this say about your need for relationship?

_____

The Lord God said, "It is not good for man to be alone. I will make a helper suitable for him." (Genesis 2:18-23)

Everything that God created, he said was "good" except that Adam had no human companion. What does this say about how important God thinks relationship is?

_____

_____

Did Adam have to take care of his needs all by himself? Who saw what his relational needs were and took care of them?

_____

SEPARATION FROM GOD

And the LORD God commanded the man, "You are free to eat from any tree in the garden; but you must not eat from the tree of the knowledge of good and evil, for when you eat from it you will certainly die." (Genesis 2:16-17)

...Now the serpent was craftier than any of the wild animals the LORD God had made. He said to the woman, "Did God really say, 'You must not eat from any tree in the garden'?" The woman said to the serpent, "We may eat fruit from the trees in the garden, but God did say, 'You must not eat fruit from the tree that is in the middle of the garden, and you must not touch it, or you will die.'" "You will not certainly die," the serpent said to the woman. "For God knows that when you eat from it your eyes will be opened, and you will be like God, knowing good and evil."

When the woman saw that the fruit of the tree was good for food and pleasing to the eye, and also desirable for gaining wisdom, she took some and ate it. She also gave some to her husband, who was with her, and he ate it. Then the eyes of both of them were opened, and they realized they were naked; so they sewed fig leaves together and made coverings for themselves. Then the man and his wife heard the sound of the LORD God as he was walking in the garden in the cool of the day, and they hid from the LORD God among the trees of the garden. But the LORD God called to the man, "Where are you?" (Genesis 3:1-8)

If God was "walking" with Adam in the Garden of Eden, what kinds of things does this show about their relationship, originally?

_____

_____

_____

As soon as Satan asked, Eve doubted what God told them. How confident was she in God, and in his relationship with them?   What caused this?

_____

_____

If Adam listened to Eve and also doubted what God had told him, what does that tell you about who he trusted in that moment?

_____

_____

Adam and Eve's relationship with God experienced a great separation as a result of their disobedience. What did they do, which showed this?

_____

_____

When they hid, what kinds of feelings went with this? How had their feelings changed about relating to God?

_____

_____

Which of these feelings can you most relate to?

_____

_____

God responded very quickly to Adam and Even when their relationship was suddenly broken. What two things did He do?

_____

_____

ENOCH WALKS WITH GOD

When Enoch had lived 65 years, he became the father of Methuselah. After he became the father of Methuselah, Enoch walked faithfully with God 300 years and had other sons and daughters. Altogether, Enoch lived a total of 365 years. Enoch *walked faithfully with God; then he was no more, because God took him up. (Genesis. 5:21-24)*

What does the Scripture say about the reason why God took Enoch to heaven?

_____

_____

What does this say about God felt about Enoch? How much did God love walking with him?

_____

_____

Does God want you to skip death too? How must He feel about you?

_____

What must you do too? Is this something you can do, or something very specific, that only a special kind of person can do?

_____

_____

How does this remind you of the Garden of Eden? Who else walked with God and experienced communion with him?

_____

_____

If Enoch fellowshipped with God on earth, what do you think Enoch did with God once he reached heaven?

_____

What does this suggest is the most important aspect of heaven? Is it comfort or riches? Or something (or Someone) else?

_____

What does this suggest is the most important thing to God, even eternally?

_____

ABRAHAM DIALOGUES WITH GOD

Abram lived in the land of Canaan, while Lot lived among the cities of the plain and pitched his tents near Sodom. Now the people of Sodom were wicked and were sinning greatly against the Lord... Then the Lord said, "Shall I hide from Abraham what I am about to do? Abraham will surely become a great and powerful nation, and all nations on earth will be blessed through him. For I have chosen him so that he will direct his children and his household after him to keep the way of the Lord by doing what is right and just, so that the Lord will bring about for Abraham what he has promised him..." (Genesis 13:8-11)

God knew Abraham cared about Sodom. Did God hide what he wanted to do—to judge the city—from Abraham?

_____

Why didn't God hide it from Abraham? What was God trying to keep?

_____

_____

If God had destroyed Sodom without telling Abraham about it, how might this have affected Abraham's faith and trust in what God had promised him earlier?

_____

_____

... The men turned and went away from Sodom but Abraham remained standing before the Lord. Then Abraham approached Him and said: "Will you sweep away the righteous with the wicked? What if there are fifty righteous people in the city? Will you really sweep it away and not spare the place for the sake of the fifty righteous people in it? Far be it from you to do such a thing—to kill the righteous with the wicked, treating the righteous and the wicked alike. Far be it from you! Will not the Judge of all the Earth do right?"

The Lord said, "If I find fifty righteous people in the city of Sodom, I will spare the whole place for their sake." Then Abraham spoke up again: "Now that I have been so bold as to speak to the Lord, though I am nothing but dust and ashes, what if the number of the righteous is five less than fifty? Will you destroy the whole city for lack of five people?" "If I find forty-five there," the Lord said, "I will not destroy it." Once again he spoke to him, "What if only forty are found there?" He said, "For the sake of forty, I will not do it."

Then he said, "May the Lord not be angry, but let me speak. What if only thirty can be found there?" He answered, "I will not do it if I find thirty there." Abraham said, "Now that I have been so bold as to speak to the Lord, what if only twenty can be found there?" He said, "For the sake of twenty, I will not destroy it." Then he said,

"May the Lord not be angry, but let me speak just once more. What if only ten can be found there?" He answered, "For the sake of ten, I will not destroy it." When the Lord had finished speaking with Abraham, He left, and Abraham returned home. (Genesis 18:16-33)

What was Abraham doing when he began a dialogue with the Lord?

_____

From how he spoke to the Lord, how do you think Abraham felt about petitioning Him? What kinds of emotions can you see?

_____

How many times did Abraham continue to ask God to change His mind?

_____

How did the Lord respond to this asking? Was He impatient?

_____

What kind of relationship does the interaction between God and Abraham show that they had?

_____

You are also a child of Abraham (Galatians 3:7, Romans 4:16-4:11, Luke 19:9). Because of this connection, what kind of relationship does God want you to have with Him?

_____

Will He be upset when you speak to Him, or ask for things on your heart?

_____

And Abraham believed God, and it was reckoned to him as righteousness, and he was called the friend of God. (James 2:23)

What word does the Bible use to describe Abraham's relationship with God?

_____

What was the main thing that made God draw close to Abraham?

_____

"I no longer call you servants, because a servant does not know his master's business. Instead, I have called you friends, for everything that I learned from my Father I have made known to you. You did not choose me, but I chose you and appointed you so that you might go and bear fruit—fruit that will last—and so that whatever you ask in my name the Father will give you." (John 15:15-16)

What does Jesus call you?

_____

What two things does God promise you, if you accept His appointing you to the "master's business"?

_____

God says three times to ask Him for what you need in the space of approximately one chapter-- John 15:7, 15:16, and 16:23-24. What kind of parent would encourage you to continually ask for things so that they can give them to you?

_____

Does God like to give? Should you feel bad when you ask Him to?

_____

God wants us to ask for the good things of heaven to come to earth. If He got His way, what do you think God imagined would result from His giving you what you ask?

_____

_____

_____

MOSES AND JOSHUA

The Lord used to speak to Moses face to face, just as a man speaks to his friend… When Moses returned to the camp, his servant Joshua, the son of Nun, a young man, would not depart from the tent." (Exodus 33:11)

What word does the Bible use to describe how God desired to talk to Moses?

_____

How do you speak to your friends? How would your life change if you spoke to God like this? Would it be easier, less lonely, or... ?

_____

_____

Scripture has a lot to say about what we believe about God, and how we feel about Him. Feelings can lead us astray at times but they can also propel us towards the things of God if they are refined!

Think of how God feels to you now, and how praying to Him feels to you. How would God feel to you if you spent a lifetime speaking to Him like a friend?

_____

_____

God initiated this relationship with Moses to tell the secrets of how to draw Israel close to Him. What does this say about how God feels about His people?

_____

_____

What did Joshua learn from watching Moses? What would have his thoughts been about how God would talk and respond?

_____

_____

Was friendship with God reserved specifically just for one special man?

_____

JESUS' DESIRE TO BEFRIEND US

I will pray to the Father, and He shall give you another Comforter, that He may abide with you forever. (John 14:16)

Of all the things God could have given us, He chose to give the Holy Spirit to "comfort" us. What does this say about God?

_____

The Holy Spirit is not just a gift. He is God himself. This means who is really doing the comforting?

_____

Oh Jerusalem, Jerusalem, you who kill the prophets and stone those sent to you, how often I have longed to gather your children together, as a hen gathers her chicks under her wings, and you were not willing. (Luke 13:34)

What kind of a relationship does a hen have with her chicks?

_____

_____

What is this saying about God's feelings towards us?

_____

_____

Jesus said this at a time when He was feeling frustrated and angry towards the Pharisees who resisted Him. This means that when we sin and resist God, is He hoping we will gather and be protected?

_____

How do you imagine this works with repentance?

_____

_____

Who runs from relationship—God, or us?

_____

Jesus wept. (John 11:35)

This is one of the most famous verses in the Bible, which Jesus does right after He learns His friend, Lazarus, has died. What does Jesus' friendship tell us about His nature? What does His crying say?

_____

_____

Is He feeling (emotional) or unfeeling (unemotional)?

_____

Are His feelings personal? Or intellectual, from a distance?

_____

Does God feel sad when we are sad? How can you tell?

_____

_____

What about when you are hurting, or when someone you love has died? Does God want you to "buck up" or explain it away theologically?

_____

_____

DRAWING CLOSE TO THE FATHER

I tell you the truth; it is better that I go away for if I do not go away, the Helper will not come to you. But if I go, I will send him to you...When the Spirit of truth comes, he will guide you into all the truth, for he will not speak on his own authority but whatever he hears he will speak, and he will declare to you the things that are to come. He will glorify me, for he will take what is mine and declare it to you. All that the Father has is mine; therefore I said that he will take what is mine and declare it to you. (John 16:7, 13-15)

Does God want you to be left alone?

_____

What about the Father Himself? Does He want to be alone?

_____

How can you tell? (Who has He always had with Him?)

_____

_____

What part of this verse tells you that the Father does not want any secrets between Himself and you?

_____

_____

_____

What part of this verse tells you that the Father does not want to hold back anything from you?

_____

_____

_____

In that day, you will ask in my name, and I do not say that I will ask the Father on your behalf; for the Father himself loves you because you have loved me and have believed that I came from God.   (John 16:26-27)

Can you pray to the Father for what you need?

_____

Do you have to worry that He is angry with you, for any reason?

_____

Does Jesus need to change the Father's mind, to keep his wrath from you?

_____

I do not ask for these only but also for those who will believe in my through their word, that they may all be one just as you, Father, are in me, and I in you, that they also may be in us, so that the world may believe that you have sent me. The glory that you have given me, I have given to them so that they may be one even as we are one. I in them and you in me, that they may become perfectly one, so that the world may know that you sent me and loved them even as you loved me. Father, I desire that they whom you have given me may also be with me where I am, to see my glory that you have given me because you loved me before the foundation of the world...I will continue to make it know that the love with which you have loved me may be in them, and I in them." (John 17:20-26).

This is a long passage because it contains one of Jesus' own prayers to the Father. Does Jesus make any distinctions between Himself, the Father, and us? Are we supposed to be separated in any way?

_____

_____

What is the main emotion circulating between God and us?

_____

_____

Does God want close relationship? How close?

_____

_____

Draw near to God and He will draw near to you. (James 4:8)

If you want God to be closer to you, what should you do?

_____

_____

REFLECTION QUESTION:

❖ What does God want from me?
    → *Do I want this?*

WEEK 1: GOD

Call to Action- Say "Yes" to Knowing God!

Main Points-

- God has a loving nature.
- We must have a heart that can receive His love.
- The Father has a deep desire for relationship.
- We were created for connection, but sin severed that connection.
- God has made us friends through Jesus.
- We must draw close to the Father.

Next Steps-

- ❖ ***Start praying*** (talking to) God. Pray through each day as if you were talking to a friend, and as if God were with you, hearing every word... because He is.
- ❖ If you are new to Christianity, start ***reading the New Testament.*** The Gospel of John is a good place to start if you need a recommendation. (If you don't have a Bible, you can download one for free on your phone.)
- ❖ Find someone who can ***mentor*** you in the faith for the next season, or contact the New Believers team who will help you. Find someone healthy who can meet with you each week, pray with you, and give you some resources to grow deeper in your faith.

Key Scripture to Meditate on:

For God so loved the world that He gave His one and only Son, that whoever believes in Him shall not perish but have everlasting life. For God did not send his Son into the world to condemn the world but to save the world through Him. (John 3:16-17)

JESUS

Salvation Through Jesus
Living in Christ

Salvation Through Jesus

THE GOSPEL

For God so loved the world that he gave his one and only Son, that whoever believes in Him shall not perish but have eternal life. For God did not send his Son into the world to condemn the world, but to save the world through Him. (John 3:16-17)

How did God feel about saving the world?

_____

What did He do, to save us?

_____

How do you receive eternal life?

_____

Is God's heart desire to punish people for their sin?

_____

What kind of love does God have?

_____

SAVED FROM SIN

Sin lost our destiny.

For all have sinned and fall short of the glory of God. (Romans 3:23)

What is our true destiny?

_____

Why can't we reach this destiny (on our own)?

_____

The Bible describes "glory" as "shining" or "radiance." What is God hoping His people will do, as bearers of His image?

_____

_____

Sin destroyed our goodness.

As it is written, "there is no-one righteous, not even one; there is no-one who understands; there is no-one who seeks God." (Romans 3:11)

Is there such thing as a truly "good person," according to Scripture?

_____

Why not? What is the true root (origin) of righteous behavior?

_____

_____

Sin causes us to reap destruction in our lives.

For the wages of sin is death, but the gift of God is eternal life in Christ Jesus our Lord. (Romans 6:23)

Why do you think God describes sin like "wages"?

_____

_____

_____

What is the ultimate consequence of sin?

_____

Is God happy about this situation? How can you tell?

_____

_____

God's loving intervention.

But God demonstrates His own love for us in this: while we were still sinners, Christ died for us. (Romans 5:8)

Does God dislike us because we sin?

_____

What was His response to sin?

_____

For this reason the Father loves Me, because I lay down My life so that I may take it up again. No one has taken it away from Me, but I lay it down on My own initiative. I have authority to lay it down, and I have authority to take it up again. This commandment I received from My Father. (John 10:17-18)

Did Jesus have a choice to accept the Cross?

_____

If Jesus hadn't suffered, who would have had to do it?

_____

For the joy set before Him, He endured the Cross, scorning its shame, and sat down at the right hand of the throne of God. (Hebrews 12:2)

How did Jesus feel about sacrificing Himself for you?

_____

Where does He sit now, advocating for you?

_____

THE RETURNING SON

[The son] got up and came to his father. But while he was still a long way off, his father saw him and felt compassion for him, and ran and embraced him and kissed him. And the son said to him, "Father, I have sinned against heaven and in your sight; I am no longer worthy to be called your son." But the father said to his slaves,

"Quickly, bring out the best robe and put it on him, and put a ring on his hand and sandals on his feet; and bring the fattened calf, kill it, and let us eat and celebrate; **for this son of mine was dead and has come to life again***; he was* **lost** *and has been* **found***." And they began to celebrate.* (Luke 15:19-24)

As a rich man, the father in this story has all he needs—except what? Why does what he's missing matter most?

_____

_____

The fattened calf would have been a farmer's most prized possession. How willing is the father, to sacrifice it for the renewed fellowship?

_____

Does the father want to punish his lost son? Or forgive him?

_____

Does the father want to think about what the son did in the past, or celebrate his new choice?

_____

What matters most to your heavenly Father, about you?

_____

Remember that you were at that time separated from Christ... having no hope and without God in the world. But now in Christ Jesus you who once were far off have been brought near by the blood of Christ. (Ephesians 2:11-13)

God cared about you when He saw that you were without what?

_____

What kind of person cares about you when you have no hope?

_____

How did God bring you near to Him again?

_____

JESUS TAKES THE PAIN

Then the high priest tore his clothes and said, "He has spoken blasphemy! Why do we need any more witnesses? Look, now you have heard the blasphemy. What do you think?" "He is **worthy of death**," they answered. Then they **spit** in His face and **struck** Him with their fists. Others **slapped** Him and said, "Prophesy to us, Messiah. Who hit you?"

When Pilate saw that he was getting nowhere, but that instead an uproar was starting, he took water and washed his hands in front of the crowd. "I am innocent of this man's blood," he said. "It is your responsibility!" All the people answered, "His blood is on us and on our children!" Then he released Barabbas to them. But he had Jesus **flogged**, and handed Him over to be crucified...

Then the governor's soldiers took Jesus into the Praetorium and gathered the whole company of soldiers around Him. They **stripped** Him and put a scarlet robe on Him, and then twisted together a crown of **thorns** and set it on His head. They put a staff in His right hand. Then they knelt in front of Him and **mocked** Him. "Hail, king of the Jews!" they said. They **spit** on Him, and took the staff and **struck** Him on the head again and again. After they had mocked Him, they took off the robe and put His own clothes on Him. Then they led Him away to **crucify** Him.

As they were going out, they met a man from Cyrene named Simon, and they forced him to [help] **carry** the cross. They came to a place called Golgotha (which means "the place of the skull"). There they offered Jesus wine to drink mixed with **gall**; but after tasting it, He refused to drink it. When they had crucified Him, they **divided up his clothes** by casting lots. And sitting down, they kept watch over Him there. Above His head they placed the written charge against Him: THIS IS JESUS, THE KING OF THE JEWS.

Two rebels were crucified with Him, one on His right and one on His left. Those who passed by **hurled insults** at Him, shaking their heads and saying, "You who are going to destroy the temple and build it in three days, save yourself! Come down from the cross, if you are the Son of God!" In the same way the chief priests, the teachers of the law and the elders **mocked** Him. "He saved others," they said, "but he can't save himself! He's the king of Israel! Let him come down now from the cross, and we will believe in him. He trusts in God. Let God rescue him now if he wants him, for he said, 'I am the Son of God.'" In the same way the rebels who were crucified with Him also **heaped insults** on Him.

From noon until three in the afternoon **darkness** came over all the land. About three in the afternoon **Jesus cried out** in a loud voice, "Eli, Eli, lema sabachthani?" (which means "My God, my God, why have you **forsaken** me?"). When some of those standing there heard this, they said, "He's calling Elijah." Immediately one of them ran and got a sponge. He filled it with wine **vinegar**, put it on a staff, and offered it to Jesus to drink. The rest said, "Now leave him alone. Let's see if Elijah comes to save him." And when Jesus had **cried out again** in a loud voice, He **gave up** His spirit.

At that moment the curtain of the temple was torn in two from top to bottom. The earth shook, the rocks split and the tombs broke open. The bodies of many holy people who had died were raised to life. They came out of the tombs after Jesus' resurrection and went into the holy city and appeared to many people. When the centurion and those with him who were guarding Jesus saw the earthquake and all that had happened, they were terrified, and exclaimed, "Surely He was the Son of God!" (Matthew 26:65-68, 27:24-54)

What kind of sacrifice did Jesus demonstrate was necessary to cover your sin? Was it quick and simple, or lengthy and painful?

_____

Take note of the different kinds of pain and torment Jesus experienced. What kinds of things did He endure to demonstrate how far He was willing to go to get you back?

_____

_____

_____

→   The Cross was Jesus suffering *with* you, through the things that come against you in this world. He identifies with your pain.

Of the kinds of pain and difficulties in this passage, which do you most relate to? Do you have anything you are hoping Jesus identifies with, that is reflected here?

_____

_____

How does it make you feel to know that God Himself still identifies and suffers with you now, in this life?

_____

_____

→   The Cross was also Jesus suffering *for* you, or *in place* of you.

If you have ever suffered because someone *else* did something wrong, what did that look like? Feel like?

_____

_____

How does it make you feel to know that you will not face death or punishment, the ultimate consequences of sin? That God has saved you from these?

_____

Surely He took up our pain and bore our suffering, yet we considered Him punished by God, stricken by him and afflicted. But He was pierced for our transgressions, He was bruised for our iniquities. The punishment that brought us peace was upon Him, and by His wounds we are healed. (Isaiah 53:4-5)

What did Jesus "take up" on the Cross?

_____

What two things did His punishment in our place purchase?

_____

_____

[Paul's jailer] brought them out and asked, "Sirs, what must I do to be saved?" They replied, "Believe in the Lord Jesus and you will be saved, you and your household." (Acts 16:30-31)

How are we saved?

_____

According to the Scriptures above, what must you believe about Jesus?

_____

_____

Salvation exists in no one else, for there is no other Name under heaven given to men by which we must be saved. (Acts 4:12)

Can any other person, religion, or way save you?

_____

→ Salvation is the most important choice we can make in this life. God has given His Son- His Name and His body- to mankind as a gift.

THE MEANING OF THE CROSS

We have new life.

When you were dead in your sins and in the uncircumcision of your sinful nature, God made you alive with Christ. He forgave us all our sins, having canceled the debt ascribed to us in the decrees that stood against us. He took it away, nailing it to the Cross! And having disarmed the powers and authorities, He made a public spectacle of them, triumphing over them by the Cross. (Colossians 2:13-15)

Jesus hung on the Cross, but what else was hung there with Him?

_____

Have you ever had a financial debt of any kind? What did it feel like?

_____

How would you feel if it were completely canceled?

_____

How would you feel about the one who canceled it?

_____

Was it God's joy to do this? How can you tell?

_____

How victorious was the Cross, in cancelling every evil thing?

_____

Jesus came to destroy the works of the devil. (1 John 3:8)

What did the Cross accomplish?

_____

And now He has made all of this plain to us by the appearing of Christ Jesus, our Savior. He broke the power of death and illuminated the way to life and immortality through the Good News. (2 Timothy 1:10)

What did Jesus' sacrifice obtain for you?

_____

Before He did that, what had power over you?

_____

We have forgiveness.

Day after day every priest stands and performs his religious duties; again and again he offers the same sacrifice, which can never take away sins. But when this Priest had offered for all time one sacrifice for sins, He sat down at the right hand of God... For by one sacrifice He has made perfect forever those who are being made holy... (Hebrews 10:11-14)

Can earthly sacrifices earn forgiveness for sin?

_____

If sacrifices can't earn forgiveness, what about the good works you do? Can those "earn" you heaven?

_____

_____

What wouldn't be fair about the ability to obtain heaven by good works?

_____

Many religions have had priests and required sacrifices since ancient times. Why did Jesus' sacrifice end all sacrificial systems, for all of time?

_____

_____

What did His sacrifice do for those who would follow Him?

_____

How does God feel towards your sins now-- is He thinking about them? Remembering them? Expecting you to make up for them?

_____

_____

We have new citizenship.

*For he has rescued us **from** the dominion of darkness and **brought us into** the kingdom of the Son he loves, in whom we have redemption, the forgiveness of sins. (Colossians 1:13-14)*

What is the nature of the new Kingdom you are part of now?

_____

Who no longer has a right to touch you? Why not?

_____

_____

For He Himself is our peace. He has made us both one and has broken down in His flesh the dividing wall of hostility, by abolishing in His flesh the enmity, which is the Law of commandments contained in ordinances, so that He might create in Himself one new man in place of the two, thus establishing peace, and might reconcile us both to God in one body through the Cross, thereby killing the hostility. (Ephesians 2:14-16)

What did the Cross abolish?

_____

In this new citizenship, is God at peace with you? Why?

_____

_____

Are you at peace with others? Why?

_____

_____

We have freedom to walk in holiness and grace.

When we lived according to the flesh, the sinful passions aroused by the law were at work in our bodies, bearing fruit for death. But now, having died to what bound us, we have been released from the law, so that we serve in the new way of the Spirit, and not in the old way of the written code. (Romans 7:5-6)

How does Jesus' work on the Cross empower us to walk in grace and holiness?

_____

_____

*My little children, I am writing these things to you so that you will not sin. But if anyone does sin, we have an **advocate** before the Father— Jesus Christ, the Righteous One. He Himself is the atoning sacrifice for our sins, and not only for ours but also for the sins of the whole world.... (1 John 2:1)*

Who advocates for you in heaven?

_____

*Christ Jesus who died--more than that, who was raised to life--is at the right hand of God and is also **interceding** for us. (Romans 8:34)*

What is Jesus doing right now?

_____

DEVOTION TO JESUS

Giving Him all

I count all things as loss compared to the surpassing excellence of knowing Christ Jesus my Lord, for whom I have lost all things. I consider them rubbish, that I may gain Christ... (Philippians 3:8)

How devoted to the Lord Jesus should we be, in our lives?

_____

What things do we tend to think are important to who we are, or how successfully our lives will go?

_____

Which of these can we hold on to?

_____

Accepting Rejection and Persecution

If the world hates you, you know that it has hated Me before it hated you. If you were of the world, the world would love its own; but because you are not of the world, but I chose you out of the world, therefore the world hates you... Remember that if they persecuted me, they will persecute you...

What two systems does Jesus present here, in this life? Are they aligned or opposed?

_____

Why do people committed to the world hate Christians?

_____

Will you always win them over? Why not?

_____

_____

Blessed are you when men cast insults at you, and persecute you, and say all kinds of evil against you falsely, on account of Me. Rejoice, and be glad, for your reward in heaven is great, for so they persecuted the prophets who were before you. (Matthew 5:11-12)

How should you feel when you are rejected on behalf of Jesus?

_____

What do you gain when you are persecuted because of your relationship with Jesus?

_____

_____

If no-one *ever* rejects you because of your beliefs, what might this mean?

_____

_____

"For I came to set a man against his father, and a daughter against her mother, and a daughter-in-law against her mother-in-law; and a man's enemies will be the

members of his household. He who loves father or mother more than Me is not worthy of Me; and he who loves son or daughter more than Me is not worthy of Me. (Matthew 10:35-37)

You may be tempted or coerced to put family relationships above your commitment to Jesus. What does Jesus say about this?

_____

He who does not take up his cross and follow after Me is not worthy of Me. He who has found his life shall lose it, and he who has lost his life for My sake shall find it. (Matthew 10:38-39)

Why does following Jesus entail "taking up our cross"?

_____

_____

Therefore everyone who confesses Me before men, I will also confess him before My Father in heaven. (Matthew 10:32)

What does God ask us, to call us His own children?

_____

What would "confessing Him before men" look like, in your life?

_____

What happens if you go back to the unbelieving world?

_____

To the one who is victorious, I will grant the right to eat from the tree of life in the paradise of God.

If we persist in God, despite the world's pressures, where will we end up in eternity?

_____

Just as man is appointed to die once, and after that to face judgment, so also Christ was offered once to bear the sins of many; and He will appear a second time, not to bear sin, but to bring salvation to those who eagerly await Him.

If you have given your life to Jesus, is the story over? What comes next?

_____

_____

Who will be saved when He returns?

_____

What kind of way do you need to live to end up "eagerly awaiting" Him?

_____

_____

REFLECTION QUESTION

❖   What is the gospel? What does it mean?
  →   *Is there anyone or anything stopping me from giving Jesus my whole heart?*

LIVING IN CHRIST

REPENTANCE

Repent, then, and turn back, so that your sins may be wiped away, that times of refreshing may come from the presence of the Lord... (Acts 3:19-20)

What is the thing you must do, to be cleansed and refreshed?

_____

Where does this cleansing and refreshing come from? What is restored to you?

_____

Zaccheus stopped and said to the Lord, "Behold, Lord, half of my possessions I will give to the poor, and if I have defrauded anyone of anything, I will give back four times as much." And Jesus said to him, "Today salvation has come to this house, because he, too, is a son of Abraham." (Luke 19:7-10)

What did Zaccheus do when he repented?

_____

_____

Why does repaying or making restitution show repentance? What does it show about the heart?

_____

_____

Is there anything God is asking you to repent of? Or any way He is asking you to make something right?

_____

_____

I count all things to be loss in view of the surpassing value of knowing Christ Jesus my Lord, for whom I have suffered the loss of all things. I count them but rubbish so that

I may gain Christ, and may be found in Him, not having a righteousness of my own derived from the Law, but that which is through faith in Christ, the righteousness which comes from God on the basis of faith. (Philippians 3:8-9)

What is the point of turning away from all the things of the world? What do you get in return?

_____

_____

Does God love and accept you because you are "good enough"? Where does your good standing (righteousness) come from?

_____

FORGIVENESS

We all stumble in many ways (James 3:2)

Does being a Christian make you perfect?

_____

If we claim to be without sin, we deceive ourselves and the truth is not in us. (1 John 1:8)

If you think you never sin or need forgiveness, what does this say?

_____

_____

I am writing this to you so that you will not sin. But if anyone does sin, we have an advocate who pleads our case before the Father. He is Jesus Christ, the one who is truly righteous. (1 John 2:1)

Is God's provision for sin a license to do it?

_____

Who will appear before the Father on your behalf when you repent from the heart?

_____

If we confess our sins, He is faithful and just to forgive us our sins and purify us from all unrighteousness. (1 John 1:9)

If you sin, what should you do?

_____

Will God forgive you?

_____

What will He also do?

_____

How does it make you feel, to know that God will forgive you if you confess?

_____

_____

Let us therefore approach God's throne of grace with confidence, so that we may receive mercy and find grace to help us in our time of need. (Hebrews 4:16)

How should you feel when you ask for forgiveness from God?

_____

What does He give us when we ask?

_____

What kind of nature must God have, to feel this way about us and ask us to approach confidently?

_____

As far as the east is from the west, so far has He removed our transgressions from us. (Psalm 103:12)

Do your stains stay? Where do they go?

_____

_____

Does God keep a record of your wrongs?

_____

For if you forgive men when they sin against you, your heavenly Father will also forgive you. But if you do not forgive men their sins, your Father will not forgive your sins. (Matthew 6:14-15)

Should you keep a record of someone else's wrongs?

_____

What is the only thing God wants in return, for the kindness He shows you?

_____

Is forgiving someone else your choice?

_____

Why do you look at the speck of sawdust in your brother's eye and pay no attention to the plank in your own eye? How can you say to your brother, 'Let me take the speck out of your eye,' when all the time there is a plank in your own eye? You hypocrite, first take the plank out of your own eye, and then you will see clearly to remove the speck from your brother's eye. (Matthew 7:3-5)

Do most people want to deal with our own faults first, or the faults of others first?

_____

Do most people tend to see their *own* faults as bigger or smaller than they really are?

_____

Do most people tend to see *others'* faults as bigger or smaller than they really are?

_____

When we examine others' faults, do we tend to see them accurately as a mix of many factors, or inaccurately and simpler than they really are? Do we see them sympathetically or unsympathetically? Circle which.

What does Jesus require us to do before we consider the faults of others?

_____

What size does Jesus say our part of the problem really is?

_____

How long do you think it would take to remove a problem of that size?

_____

> ➤ If there is anyone you currently feel critical of, take a moment to list them here and why. Then list a few ways that you could show the love of Jesus to them.
> ➤ Pray and ask Jesus if there are any logs in your own eye that He wants you to deal with before your remove the specks from those people you wrote down.

Blessed are the merciful, for they will be shown mercy. (Matthew 5:7)

WATER BAPTISM

*Jesus came to them and said, "All authority in heaven and on earth has been given to Me. Therefore go and make disciples of all nations, **baptizing** them in the name of the Father, and of the Son, and of the Holy Spirit, and teaching them to obey all that I have commanded you. (Matthew 28:18-19; also Mark 16:16)*

What sign did Jesus say should accompany conversion and belief in Him?

_____

What is a baptized believer then on the path to doing?

_____

In Him you were also circumcised with a circumcision not performed by human hands. Your whole self ruled by the flesh was put off when you were circumcised by Christ, having been buried with Him in baptism, in which you were also raised with

Him through your faith in the working of God, who raised Him from the dead. (Colossians 2:11-12)

What is the "circumcision" of Christ?

_____

When you are baptized, what does it show you are "putting off" or "burying"?

_____

What future act does it symbolize is coming?

_____

We were therefore buried with Him through baptism into death, in order that, just as Christ was raised from the dead through the glory of the Father, we too may walk in newness of life. (Romans 6:4)

Baptism is a symbolic burial and resurrection. What do we walk in, when we come up out of the water?

_____

What is gone?

_____

YOUR NEW IDENTITY

But as many as received Him, to them He gave power to become sons of God, even to them that believe on his name: Which were born, not of blood, nor of the will of the flesh, nor of the will of man, but of God. (John 1:12-13)

Jesus was the only begotten Son of God, but what does this say He gives you the power to be also?

_____

Think about what it means to be a child of a parent, here on earth. What kind of things come with being a child of God?

_____

For you died, and your life is now hidden with Christ in God. When Christ, who is our life, is revealed, then you also will be revealed with Him in glory. (Colossians 3:4)

How have you "died?"

_____

If your life is hidden, whose life is God looking at instead?

_____

If God sees you the same way he sees Jesus, then how does he see you? What was Jesus like?

_____

_____

But the one who joins himself to the Lord is one spirit with Him. (1 Corinthians 6:17)

Whose nature do you now share?

_____

What do you have to do, to keep the Lord's righteousness as your own?

_____

_____

But as many as received Him, to them He gave the right to become sons of God, even to those who believe in His name. (John 1:12)

If you have been born again, what are you now?

_____

Who used to be your father? Who is your Father now?

_____

Therefore if anyone is in Christ, he is a new creature; the old things passed away; behold, new things have come! (2 Corinthians 5:17)

Whose nature is now living inside of you?

_____

If you have the nature of Christ inside of you, what does that mean about any mistakes or challenges in your past?

_____

_____

Knowing this, that our old self was crucified with Him, in order that our body of sin might be done away with, so that we would no longer be slaves to sin. (Romans 6:6)

Are you destined to struggle with addictions or bad habits? Why not?

_____

_____

Once you were alienated from God and were enemies in your minds because of your evil behavior. But now he has reconciled you by Christ's physical body through death to present you holy in his sight, without blemish and free from accusation, established and firm. (Colossians 1:21-22)

Do you have to submit to alienating or tormenting thoughts anymore?

_____

God raised us up with Christ and seated us with Him in the heavenly places in Christ Jesus, in order that in the coming ages He might show the incomparable riches of his grace, expressed in his kindness to us in Christ Jesus. (Ephesians 2:6-8)

Where are you seated? Is this where you will be in the future, or where you are now?

_____

_____

Imagine this now for just a moment. Close your eyes. What is it like, to be seated with Him?

_____

Put on the new man, which after God is created in righteousness and true holiness. (Ephesians 4:24)

Does the Bible tell you to just try harder, when you fail?

_____

What does this Scripture tell you to do, instead?

_____

But you are a chosen people, a royal priesthood, a holy nation, God's special possession, that you may declare the praises of him who called you out of darkness into his wonderful light.

Are you special? How special are you?

_____

_____

_____

You have come out of darkness into His marvelous light—describe what you imagine that to mean, for you personally.

_____

_____

_____

HEARING GOD

"He who has ears to hear, let him hear!" (Mt. 11:15, 13:9, 13:43; Mk. 4:9, Mk. 4:23, Lk. 8:8, Lk. 14:35)

Is God talking about physical hearing? What is He talking about?

_____

_____

Jesus says this same thing in at least seven different verses. Why do you think this hearing is so important?

_____

If two people receive the same teaching, what is the difference between someone who "hears" it and someone who doesn't?

_____

_____

My sheep hear my voice, and I know them, and they follow me. *(John 10:27)*

What does God promise His followers?

_____

Do you have to worry that you don't hear God?

_____

What kinds of things might a shepherd "say" or communicate to his sheep?

_____

_____

Do sheep have to understand human language in order to know what their shepherd is telling them? Why not—how do they know?

_____

_____

WHERE POWER COMES FROM

Greater is He that is in me, than he that is in the world. (1 John 4:4)

What two systems on earth are there? Who are the leaders of those systems?

_____

_____

Are these systems compatible or opposed?

_____

Which one is meant to overcome?

_____

For I am convinced that neither death, nor life, nor angels, nor principalities, nor things present, nor things to come, nor powers, nor height, nor depth, nor any other created thing, will be able to separate us from the love of God, which is in Christ Jesus our Lord. (Romans 8:38-39)

When you're dealing with something hard—depression, failure, sin that's hard to beat—does it mean God withdraws from you?

_____

Can you do anything to stop God's love over your life? Name any you have believed have hindered it, and then cross them out.

_____

_____

_____

In all these things, we are more than conquerors through Him who loved us. (Romans 8:37)

When you face trials, who will win?

_____

What kind of attitude is God encouraging you to have, if you are "more than a conqueror"?

_____

I can do all things through Christ who gives me strength. (Philippians 4:13)

Is there anything you cannot do, if you abide in Christ?

_____

And these signs shall follow them that believe; In my name shall they cast out devils; they shall speak with new tongues; They shall take up serpents; and if they drink any deadly thing, it shall not hurt them; they shall lay hands on the sick, and they shall recover. (Mark 16:16-18)

What has God called you to do, with the power He gives you?

_____

_____

What if you face something demonic? Should you be afraid? Who has the power in those kinds of battles?

_____

_____

What about death, sickness, or torment? Who has the power over those?

_____

The thief comes to steal, to kill, and to destroy. I came so that they might have life and have it more abundantly. (John 10:10).

How can you tell if something is the work of God or the work of Satan?

_____

_____

Did Jesus come just so we could just escape the hardest forms of pain in life and get into heaven as quickly as possible?

_____

_____

Whatever you ask in My name, that will I do, so that the Father may be glorified in the Son. If you ask Me anything in My name, I will do it.   (John 14:13-14)

What will God give you if you ask?

_____

_____

Do you see any special qualifications here?

_____

_____

This is the confidence we have in approaching God: that if we ask anything according to his will, he hears us. (1 John 5:14)

How does God want you to approach Him?

_____

Does God want you to ask Him for what you need?

_____

Have you ever felt like God didn't hear your prayers? Because you are in Christ, what are you promised?

_____

_____

If you remain in me and my words remain in you, ask whatever you wish, and it will be done for you. (John 15:7)

What is the condition to receiving answers to prayer, and power in God?

_____

_____

What can you ask for, if you are in Him?

_____

_____

My prayer is not for them alone. I pray also for those who will believe in me through their message, that all of them may be one, Father, just as you are in me and I am in you. May they also be in us so that the world may believe that you have sent me. I have given them the glory that you gave me, that they may be one as we are one—I in them and you in me—so that they may be brought to complete unity. (John 17:20-23)

Are you alone anymore? Who is in you? Who are you "in"?

_____

In terms of relationship, what is the end result of following God?

_____

_____

I am the true vine, and my Father is the gardener. He cuts off every branch in me that bears no fruit, while every branch that does bear fruit he prunes so that it will be even more fruitful. You are already clean because of the word I have spoken to you. Remain in me, as I also remain in you. No branch can bear fruit by itself; it must remain in the vine. Neither can you bear fruit unless you remain in me. (John 15:1-4)

How connected does Jesus want to be?

_____

_____

Do you have to try hard to bear fruit? What enables you to bear good fruit?

_____

_____

Based on this, are we to focus more on doing good works, or on knowing Jesus better?

_____

How can trying to do good works become a trap?

_____

_____

_____

I am the vine; you are the branches. If you remain in me and I in you, you will bear much fruit; apart from me you can do nothing. If you do not remain in me, you are like a branch that is thrown away and withers; such branches are picked up, thrown into the fire and burned. If you remain in me and my words remain in you, ask whatever you wish, and it will be done for you. This is to my Father's glory, that you bear much fruit, showing yourselves to be my disciples. (John 15:5-8)

Is there anything good you can do apart from Jesus?

_____

How often does Jesus want to be with you?

_____

Is bearing fruit just good for God, or is it good for you too?

_____

REFLECTION QUESTIONS

❖ How do I feel about having Jesus with me all day, all the time, in everything I do?

❖ Do I need to make any changes to allow Him to be this close to me?

WEEK 2: SALVATION THROUGH JESUS

Call to Action- Say "Yes" to making Jesus your Lord, King and Savior. Consider being baptized if you have not been baptized before, or desire to be again.

Main Points-

- Sin destroyed our relationship with the Father.
- Jesus came to remedy that disconnection.
- He paid for our sin by His death on the Cross.
- When we accept His death and make Him our Lord, He cleans us and makes us right before the Father again.
- We then continue to live for Jesus, giving up our old ways.
- We walk holy, as children of God, and step into a life that looks more and more like His.

Next Steps-

- ❖ If you have not been baptized, or desire to be **baptized** again as a believer, please tell the leader of this class so we can help you take this step! (Water baptism is discussed in the above chapter, "Living In Christ.")
- ❖ Consider downloading the free **365 Bible app** for your phone. It offers daily Bible reading plans, with note-taking ability, as well as online devotionals and studies to choose from.
- ❖ If you have recently accepted Jesus as your Savior, find someone who can **mentor** you in the faith for the next season, or contact the New Believers team who will help you.

Key Scripture to Meditate on:

I count all things as loss compared to the surpassing excellence of knowing Christ Jesus my Lord, for whom I have lost all things. I consider them rubbish, that I may gain Christ... (Philippians 3:8)

THE HOLY SPIRIT

Who the Holy Spirit Is
Walking in the Spirit

THE HOLY SPIRIT

WHO IS THE HOLY SPIRIT?

The Father's Promised Gift

*On one occasion, while [Jesus] was eating with [His disciples], He gave them this command: "Do not leave Jerusalem, but wait **for the gift my Father promised,** which you have heard Me speak about. For John baptized with water, but in a few days you will be baptized with the Holy Spirit... you will receive power when the Holy Spirit comes on you; and you will be My witnesses in Jerusalem, and in all Judea and Samaria, and to the ends of the earth. (Acts 1:4-8)*

*And behold, I am sending **the promise of my Father** upon you. But stay in the city until you are clothed with power from on high. (Luke 24:49)*

Who originated the idea of the Holy Spirit?

_____

Was the Holy Spirit always dwelling with (saved) believers?

_____

What did Jesus say the coming of the Holy Spirit was fulfilling?

_____

What was the Holy Spirit supposed to bring, when He came?

_____

What supposed to happen after that was received?

_____

Who is with us, fulfilling the Great Commission and bringing to completion the good work that God started with Eden?

_____

So I say to you: Ask and it will be given to you; seek and you will find; knock and the door will be opened to you. For everyone who asks receives; the one who seeks finds; and to the one who knocks, the door will be opened. Which of you fathers, if your son asks for a fish, will give him a snake instead? Or if he asks for an egg, will give him a scorpion? If you then who are evil, know how to give good gifts to your children, how much more will the Heavenly Father give the Holy Spirit to those who ask him! (Luke 11:9-13)

What does your heavenly Father greatly desire to give you, as His personal gift?

_____

What is He hoping you will seek and ask for? Will it be a good gift?

_____

Would you ever give a bad gift to your children?

_____

Who does the Father give the Holy Spirit to?

_____

Our Helper and Guide

And I will ask the Father, and he will give you another Helper to be with you forever... (John 14:16)

What is the Holy Spirit's nature?

_____

When the Spirit of truth comes, he will guide you into all truth. (John 16:13)

Can your intellect alone discover truth? Who do you need to help you?

_____

_____

When they deliver you over, do not be anxious how you are to speak or what you are to say, for what you are to say will be given to you in that hour. For it is not you who speak, but the Spirit of your Father speaking through you. (Matthew 10:19-20)

If you get into a difficult situation, who will help you speak?

_____

Whose voice does the Holy Spirit reflect?

_____

The Spirit helps us in our weakness. We do not know what we ought to pray for, but the Spirit himself intercedes for us through groaning too deep for words. And he who searches our hearts knows the mind of the Spirit, because the Spirit intercedes for God's people in accordance with the will of God. (Romans 8:26-27)

How does this verse say the Holy Spirit helps us?

_____

_____

What if you don't know what to pray for? Or what God's will is when you pray?

_____

What two things does the Holy Spirit know?

_____

_____

If you have been to a formal church, you might think of prayer as something very professional—but how much emotion would you imagine is involved in "groaning too deep for words"?

_____

RECEIVING THE HOLY SPIRIT

I [John the Baptist] baptize you with water for repentance, but He who is coming after me is mightier than I, whose sandals I am not worthy to carry. He will baptize you with the Holy Spirit and with fire. (Matthew 3:11)

What did John the Baptist promise that Jesus would do?

_____

What is the nature of *fire*?

_____

Why do you think the baptism of the Spirit is likened to fire, in comparison to John's baptism with water?

_____

_____

The First Outpouring

When the day of Pentecost came, they were all together in one place. Suddenly a sound like the blowing of a violent wind came from heaven and filled the whole house where they were sitting. They saw what seemed to be tongues of fire that separated and came to rest on each of them. **All of them were filled with the Holy Spirit** *and began to speak in other tongues as the Spirit enabled them...*

Amazed and perplexed, they asked one another, "What does this mean?" Some, however, made fun of them and said, "They have had too much wine." Then Peter stood up with the Eleven, raised his voice and addressed the crowd: "Fellow Jews and all of you who live in Jerusalem, let me explain this to you; listen carefully to what I say. These people are not drunk, as you suppose. It's only nine in the morning! No, this is what was spoken by the prophet Joel:

'In the last days, God says, I will pour out my Spirit on all people. Your sons and daughters will prophesy, your young men will see visions, your old men will dream dreams. Even on my servants, both men and women, **I will pour out my Spirit in those days**, *and they will prophesy... And everyone who calls on the name of the Lord will be saved...' Therefore let all Israel be assured of this: God has made this Jesus, whom you crucified, both Lord and Messiah."*

When the people heard this, they were cut to the heart and said to Peter and the other apostles, "Brothers, what shall we do?" Peter replied, "Repent and be baptized, every one of you, in the name of Jesus Christ for the forgiveness of your sins. **And you will receive the gift of the Holy Spirit**. *The promise is for you and your children and for all who are far off—for all whom the Lord our God will call." With many other words he warned them, and he pleaded with them, "Save yourselves from this corrupt generation." Those who accepted his message were baptized, and about three thousand were added to their number that day.*

What happened when the Holy Spirit was first poured out on believers? What did it look and sound like?

_____

_____

Did everyone recognize that this was the power of God? What did those who didn't believe in it say?

_____

_____

Just 40 days before, Peter had been too afraid to admit that he was Jesus' disciple. Does he look afraid here? How did the Holy Spirit change him?

_____

According to Peter and the prophet Joel, what kinds of signs accompany the pouring out of the Holy Spirit?

_____

When the listeners asked Peter what they should do, what did he tell them? What was the result of his message?

_____

_____

Was the Holy Spirit just a sign for first-century Jerusalem? Whom did Peter say the Holy Spirit was for?

_____

_____

Do you think people need the Holy Spirit today? Why?

_____

_____

Other Examples

*And it happened that while Apollos was at Corinth, Paul passed through the inland country and came to Ephesus. There he found some disciples. And he said to them, **"Did you receive the Holy Spirit when you believed**?" And they said, "No, we have not even heard that there is a Holy Spirit." And he said, "Into what then were you baptized?" They said, "Into John's baptism." And Paul said, "John baptized with the baptism of repentance, telling the people to believe in the One who was to come after him, that is, Jesus." On hearing this, they were baptized in the name of the Lord Jesus. And when Paul had laid his hands on them, **the Holy Spirit came on them**, and they began speaking in tongues and prophesying. (Acts 19:1-6)*

The Ephesians had already been converted to Christ by the time Paul arrived there. What had they done, to show this?

_____

Why had they not yet received the gift of the Holy Spirit?

_____

_____

How did Paul impart the Holy Spirit to them?

_____

How was Paul able to tell that they had received the Spirit?

_____

Now when the apostles at Jerusalem heard that Samaria had received the word of God, they sent to them Peter and John, who came down and prayed for them that they might receive the Holy Spirit, for He had not yet fallen on any of them, but they had only been baptized in the name of the Lord Jesus. Then they laid their hands on them and they received the Holy Spirit. (Acts 8:14-17)

Can people be saved without being baptized in the Holy Spirit?

_____

Did the believers in Samaria receive the Holy Spirit on their own? What had to happen?

_____

_____

GIFTS OF THE SPIRIT

Gifts followed Jesus' resurrection.

*But grace was given to each one of us according to the measure of Christ's gift. Therefore it says, "When He ascended on high He led a host of captives, and **He gave gifts to men**"... to equip the saints for the work of ministry, for the building up of the Body of Christ. (Ephesians 4:7-11)*

Who gave the church spiritual gifts?

_____

What is the purpose of spiritual gifts?

_____

What would an "edified" or built up church look like? What could it do?

_____

Different Kinds of Gifts

We have different gifts, according to the grace given to each of us. If your gift is prophesying, then prophesy in accordance with your faith; if it is serving, then serve; if it is teaching, then teach; if it is to encourage, then give encouragement; if it is giving, then give generously; if it is leading, do it diligently; if it is to show mercy, do it cheerfully. (Romans 12:6-8)

What would a church be like if its people were full of these gifts?

_____

How do these qualities describe Jesus?

_____

→ Each gift of the Spirit expresses one quality of the complete love of God, and of the community He wants to build.

To one there is given through the Spirit a message of wisdom, to another a message of knowledge by means of the same Spirit, to another faith by the same Spirit, to another gifts of healing by that one Spirit, to another miraculous powers, to another prophecy, to another distinguishing between spirits, to another speaking in different kinds of tongues, and to still another the interpretation of tongues. All these are the work of one and the same Spirit, and He distributes them to each one, just as He determines... (1 Corinthians 12:8-11)

God has placed in the church first of all apostles, second prophets, third teachers, then miracles, then gifts of healing, of helping, of guidance, and of different kinds of tongues. (1 Corinthians 12:28)

Does God expect the church to be a miraculous Body?

_____

Do only pastors or leaders have gifts, or does the whole Body? Do only a few have gifts?

_____

Why don't we all have the same experiences in the Holy Spirit?

_____

Now about the gifts of the Spirit, brothers and sisters, I do not want you to be uninformed... There are different kinds of gifts, but the same Spirit distributes them. There are different kinds of service, but the same Lord. There are different kinds of working, but in all of them and in everyone it is the same God at work. (1 Corinthians 12:1, 4-6)

Are gifts meant to be divisive? Or in competition with one another?

_____

Whose will is supposed to be operating behind all the gifts?

_____

Love and Edification in the Church

Now to each one the manifestation of the Spirit is given for the common good... (1 Corinthians 12:7)

What is the purpose of the Holy Spirit's presence in church?

_____

Does everyone have a spiritual gift?

_____

Is it publicly visible?

_____

Speaking the truth in love, we are to grow up in every way into Him who is the head, into Christ, from whom the whole Body, joined and held together by every joint with which it is equipped, when each part is working properly, makes the Body grow so that it builds itself up in love. (Ephesians 4:15-16)

72

Is the Holy Spirit's intention to make us strange or off-putting?

_____

What should always be the motivating force behind operating in spiritual gifts?

_____

Are some gifts more valuable than others?

_____

What happens when all God's gifts are working together, in concert and in humility with one another?

_____

_____

Going Deeper

*Now eagerly **desire** the greater gifts... (1 Corinthians 12:31)*

*Follow the way of love and **pursue** gifts of the Spirit... (1 Corinthians 14:1)*

Can you ask God for more spiritual gifts?

_____

Can you acquire more of them, or a greater measure of one?

_____

Why does God want you to pursue gifts--to promote what?

_____

WALKING BY THE SPIRIT

*So I say, **walk by the Spirit,** and you will not gratify the desires of the flesh. For the flesh desires what is contrary to the Spirit, and the Spirit what is contrary to the flesh. They are in conflict with each other, so that you are not to do what you want... (Galatians 5:16-17)*

According to the Bible, what two forces are going on within a person?

_____

Now the acts of the flesh are obvious: sexual immorality, impurity and debauchery; idolatry and witchcraft; hatred, discord, jealousy, fits of rage, selfish ambition, dissensions, factions and envy; drunkenness, orgies, and the like. I warn you, as I did before, that those who live like this will not inherit the kingdom of God. But the fruit of the Spirit is love, joy, peace, forbearance, kindness, goodness, faithfulness, gentleness and self-control. (Gal. 5:18-22)

What two kinds of fruit do people produce?

_____

Why would God compare the evidence of the Holy Spirit to fruit?

_____

_____

How can you tell if you are operating in the Holy Spirit correctly?

_____

_____

Keeping in step with the Spirit

Those who belong to Christ Jesus have crucified the flesh with its passions and desires. Since we live by the Spirit, let us keep in step with the Spirit. (Gal. 5:24-25)

How do we produce more of the good fruit we want?

_____

What does "keeping in step" with the Holy Spirit imply about his movement?

_____

_____

Abide in me, as I abide in you. No branch can bear fruit by itself; it must **remain** in the vine. Neither can you bear fruit unless you remain in me. *(John 15:4)*

What must we always do, to bear spiritual fruit?

_____

_____

→   The Holy Spirit is "holy"! He works in us to do God's will and edify the Body of which Jesus is the head.

REFLECTION QUESTION:

❖   Why did God send the Holy Spirit to His children?
    →   *Do I need this too?*

WALKING IN THE SPIRIT

THE GOD WHO SPEAKS

You know that when you were pagans, you were influenced and led astray to mute idols. (1 Corinthians 12:2)

If idols are "mute," then what is the real God?

_____

→ God has a voice and He uses it! The essence of God is His voice because He is a spirit, and invisible. With His voice comes His presence, as well as His thoughts, plans, desires. He's a communicating God. He communicates because His heart is to be with us, and have us with Him.

Then the Lord called Samuel. Samuel answered, "Here I am." And he ran to Eli and said, "Here I am; you called me." But Eli said, "I did not call; go back and lie down." So he went and lay down. Again the Lord called, "Samuel!" And Samuel got up and went to Eli and said, "Here I am; you called me." "My son," Eli said, "I did not call; go back and lie down." Now Samuel did not yet know the Lord: The word of the Lord had not yet been revealed to him. A third time the Lord called, "Samuel!" And Samuel got up and went to Eli and said, "Here I am; you called me."

Then Eli realized that the Lord was calling the boy. So Eli told Samuel, "Go and lie down, and if he calls you, say, 'Speak, Lord, for your servant is listening.' " So Samuel went and lay down in his place. The Lord came and stood there, calling as at the other times, "Samuel! Samuel!" Then Samuel said, "Speak, for your servant is listening." (1 Samuel 3:4-10)

Did God reach out to Samuel first, or did Samuel reach out to God first?

_____

Did God choose someone particularly old and wise to speak to? Or someone inexperienced but willing?

_____

Did God give up on speaking to Samuel just because he didn't understand Him the first time?

_____

How did Samuel respond when he finally realized it was God? What did God want to hear, before He spoke more?

_____

_____

What does God want from us?

_____

Did Samuel need help to discern the voice of the Lord? Is it ok if you do?

_____

As Moses went into the tent, the pillar of cloud would come down and stay at the entrance while the Lord spoke with Moses... The Lord would speak to Moses face to face, as one speaks to a friend... (Exodus 33:9-11)

What is the ultimate goal of communing with Jesus, or spending time with Him?

_____

How do friends normally speak to one another? How often do they usually speak?

_____

_____

How is reading your Bible similar to speaking to God "face to face, as one speaks to a friend?"

_____

_____

How is praying similar to speaking to God "face to face, as one speaks to a friend?"

_____

_____

*"He calls his own sheep by name and leads them out. When he has brought out all his own, he goes on ahead of them, and his sheep **follow** him because they know his*

voice. But they will never follow a stranger; in fact, they will run away from him because they do not recognize a stranger's voice. (John 10:3-5)

Does God know your name?

_____

Why does He call you?

_____

Whose voice has He made you to hear and follow?

_____

What should you do when you hear another unlike Him speaking?

_____

"But when he, the Spirit of truth, comes, he will guide you into all the truth. He will not speak on his own; he will speak only what he hears, and he will tell you what is yet to come." (John 16:13)

What is God's special gift to His children, so they can hear what He says?

_____

Why is the voice of the Holy Spirit reliable, in contrast to our own voice or another's?

_____

_____

THE GIFT OF PROPHECY

→ God desires to communicate with us. Prophecy is one of the ways He does that, through the Holy Spirit.

The Spirit searches all things, even the deep things of God. For who knows a person's thoughts except their own spirit within them? In the same way no one knows the thoughts of God except the Spirit of God. (1 Corinthians 2:10-11)

The purpose of New Testament prophecy is to disclose what two things?

_____

_____

How does prophecy act as a connector of people and God?

_____

To one there is given through the Spirit a word of wisdom, to another a word of knowledge by means of the same Spirit, to another faith by the same Spirit, to another gifts of healing by that one Spirit, to another miraculous powers, to another prophecy, to another distinguishing between spirits, to another speaking in different kinds of tongues, and to still another the interpretation of tongues." (1 Corinthians 12:8-10)

What kinds of things did God envision going on in a believing community?

_____

_____

How many of these things sound like prophecy or supernatural ways of God speaking? Underline them in the passage.

_____

What does God giving us "words of knowledge" or "wisdom" tell us about His nature?

_____

_____

Now you are the Body of Christ, and each one of you is a part of it. And God has placed in the church first of all apostles, second prophets, third teachers, then miracles, then gifts of healing, of helping, of guidance, and of different kinds of tongues." (1 Corinthians 12:27-28)

Have the roles of apostles and teachers died out? What about the gifts of helping or guidance?

_____

Is prophecy obsolete? Did it die out with Christ and the apostles?

_____

The one who prophesies speaks to people for their strengthening, encouraging and comfort. (1 Corinthians 14:3)

What *is* prophesying?

_____

Is it about predicting the End Times or cataclysmic doom? Why not?

_____

_____

Anyone who speaks in a tongue edifies themselves, but the one who prophesies edifies the church. I would like every one of you to speak in tongues, but I would rather have you prophesy. (1 Corinthians 14:4-5)

Is prophecy for today?

_____

Is it desirable? Why—what is it for?

_____

Is it for everyone? Is it for you?

_____

Now eagerly desire the greater gifts. (1 Corinthians 12:31)

*Follow the way of love and pursue gifts of the Spirit, especially prophecy… For you can **all** prophesy in turn so that everyone may be instructed and encouraged. (1 Corinthians 14:1)*

If you "eagerly desired" spiritual gifts, and "pursued" them, what would this look like in your day, your life?

_____

_____

Are there any changes you would have to make in your time, attention, resources?

_____

Did God predestine you to have just one gift you didn't choose, or can you achieve other spiritual gifts in your lifetime?

_____

Did God envision prophecy being restricted to a special class of people?

_____

How does prophecy "follow the way of love?"

_____

_____

THE PASTORAL PROPHETIC

→ The pastoral mode of prophecy which is so well described in the New Testament begins with God in the Garden of Eden. We model ourselves on the Father's example, starting in the beginning when the first pastoral moment occurred.

*Then the man and his wife heard the **sound** of the LORD God walking in the garden in the cool of the day, and the man and his wife hid themselves from the presence of the LORD God among the trees of the garden. Then the LORD God **called** to the man, and said to him, "Where are you?" Adam **answered**, "I **heard** you in the garden, and I was afraid because I was naked; so I hid." And the LORD said, "Who told you that you were naked? Have you eaten from the tree that I commanded you not to eat from?" (Genesis 3:8-11)*

After Adam and Eve hid, God spoke the first "word of knowledge" in the Bible. What was it?

_____

What was this word of knowledge meant to do? What is God's attitude about our relationship with him?

_____

_____

Throughout Scripture, God's *voice* indicates His presence. Could Adam and Eve hear it, even after they sinned?

_____

What does this mean for you? For the lost?

_____

When Jesus saw Nathanael approaching, He said of him, 'Here truly is an Israelite in whom there is no deceit.' 'How do you know me?' Nathanael asked. Jesus answered, 'I saw you while you were still under the fig tree before Philip called you.' Then Nathanael declared, 'Rabbi, you are the Son of God; you are the king of Israel.' (John 1:47-49)

Had Nathanael met Jesus before this moment?

_____

How did Jesus "see" Nathanael earlier?

_____

What revelation did Nathanael receive in return, after Jesus gave His?

_____

What was Jesus' prophetic declaration about Nathanael's identity? Was it positive or negative in tone?

_____

_____

He [Jesus] told her [the woman at the well], "Go, call your husband and come back." "I have no husband," she replied. Jesus said to her, 'You are right when you say you have no husband. The fact is, you have had five husbands, and the man you now have is not your husband. What you have just said is quite true.' 'Sir,' the woman said, 'I can see that you are a prophet.'" (John 4:16-19)

Jesus had a word of knowledge about the woman's five husbands. What did this word release her to see about herself?

_____

What did it show her about God?

_____

Do you think the woman felt judged by Jesus' revelation? What was Jesus' purpose in prophesying to her?

_____

Now a man named Ananias, together with his wife Sapphira, also sold a piece of property. With his wife's full knowledge he kept back part of the money for himself, but brought the rest and put it at the apostles' feet. Then Peter said, "Ananias, how is it that Satan has so filled your heart that you have lied to the Holy Spirit and have kept for yourself some of the money you received for the land? Didn't it belong to you before it was sold? And after it was sold, wasn't the money at your disposal? What made you think of doing such a thing? You have not lied just to human beings but to God. (Acts 5:1-5)

Did anyone know the truth of what Ananias and Sapphira did?

_____

Who received this word of knowledge? Was Jesus the only one whom the Holy Spirit could reveal things to?

_____

Ananias and Sapphira were presenting a certain amount of charity as an act of the Holy Spirit before the Christian community. Whom were they lying to? Who revealed their lie?

_____

_____

How can a prophetic act protect a church community?

_____

_____

Following after Paul and us, she kept crying out, saying, 'These men are bond-servants of the Most High God, who are proclaiming to you the way of salvation.' She continued doing this for many days. But Paul was greatly annoyed, and turned and said to the spirit, 'I command you in the name of Jesus Christ to come out of her!' And it came out at that very moment. (Acts 16:17-18)

How can a prophetic word restore order to the church?

_____

_____

Paul and his companions traveled throughout the region of Phrygia and Galatia, having been kept by the Holy Spirit from preaching the word in the province of Asia. When they came to the border of Mysia, they tried to enter Bithynia, but the Spirit of Jesus would not allow them to. So they passed by Mysia and went down to

Troas. During the night Paul had a vision of a man of Macedonia standing and begging him, "Come over to Macedonia and help us." After Paul had seen the vision, we got ready at once to leave for Macedonia, concluding that God had called us to preach the gospel to them. (Acts 16:6-10)

What word of knowledge did the Holy Spirit reveal to Paul as he planned his mission trips?

_____

_____

How can prophecy aid one's plans, calling, or the ministry God wants to do?

_____

_____

If the whole church comes together and everyone speaks in tongues, and inquirers or unbelievers come in, will they not say that you are out of your mind? But if an unbeliever or an inquirer comes in while everyone is prophesying, they are convicted of sin and are brought under judgment by all as the secrets of their hearts are laid bare. So they will fall down and worship God, exclaiming "God is really among you!" (1 Corinthians 14:23-25)

What spiritual gift can speak well to unbelievers? Why?

_____

_____

What is the effect of prophecy done well in the Body of Christ?

_____

_____

Therefore my brothers and sisters, be eager to prophesy and do not forbid speaking in tongues. But everything should be done in a fitting and orderly way. (1 Corinthians 14:39-40).

Paul believes everyone can express their spiritual gifts in church, but asks that this be done humbly, in what way?

_____

Did the Lord design prophecy do be divisive or controversial in the church?

Did he intend for people's lives to be led irrationally, etc.?

_____

SPEAKING IN THE SPIRIT

And they were all filled with the Holy Spirit and began to speak in other tongues as the Spirit gave them utterance. (Acts 2: 2-4)

What was the specific sign that the Holy Spirit had come to the first church?

_____

*While Peter was still saying these things, the Holy Spirit **fell on** all who heard the word. And the believers from among the circumcised who had come with Peter were amazed, because the gift of the Holy Spirit was **poured out** even on the Gentiles. For they were hearing them speaking in tongues and praising God. Then Peter declared, "Can anyone withhold water for baptizing these people, who have received the Holy Spirit just as we have?" And he commanded them to be baptized in the name of Jesus Christ. (Acts 10:44-48)*

How did the Gentiles receive the Holy Spirit?

_____

What two signs showed that they had received the gift?

_____

Did the new Gentile believers have to get water baptized or do other things before receiving the Holy Spirit?

_____

Was water baptism here a distinct experience from receiving the Spirit?

_____

Paul says, "I would like every one of you to speak in tongues..." (1 Corinthians 14:5)

Is praying in tongues only for a few, select people?

Anyone who speaks in a tongue edifies themselves. (1 Corinthians 14:4)

What is the benefit of praying in tongues?

_____

Can anyone do this?

_____

*Anyone who speaks in a tongue does not speak to people but to God. Indeed, no one understands them; they utter **mysteries** by the Spirit." (1 Corinthians 14:2)*

*If you speak a **blessing** in the Spirit, how can someone who is uninstructed say "Amen" to your **thanksgiving**, since he does not know what you are saying? (1 Corinthians 14:16)*

Are tongues usually understood by people? Who is being spoken to?

_____

What three things are mentioned here as things you are praying when you pray in tongues?

_____

_____

If I pray in a tongue, my spirit prays but my mind is unfruitful. (1 Corinthians 14:14)

If your mind is not edified by praying in tongues, what part of you is edified?

_____

Paul concludes, "I thank God that I speak in tongues more than all of you..." (1 Corinthians 14:18)

How much should you pray in tongues? Is it supposed to be a one-time experience?

_____

GOD'S WILL FOR HEALING

I am the Lord who heals you. (Exodus 15:26)

Many people believe that God gives them illness to teach them things, or that He "allows" them to be sick. On the contrary, what does this verse say about God's nature?

_____

Could God have said this honestly, if He desires to place sickness on people, for any reason? Why not?

_____

_____

Heal the sick, raise the dead, cure those with leprosy, and cast out demons. Freely you have received, so freely give. (Matthew 10:8)

What four groups were the disciples told to go and pray for?

_____

_____

Would Jesus have told His followers to do something they couldn't do?

_____

Would He have told them to do something that wasn't His will? Or that was only *sometimes* His will?

_____

*And God has placed **in the church** first of all apostles, second prophets, third teachers, then miracles, then gifts of **healing**, of helping, of guidance, and of different kinds of tongues. (1 Corinthians 12:28)*

Where did God want His power of healing to rest/live, after Jesus left?

_____

Does God make healing sound like a fantastical gift, out of proportion with the other gifts in the church?

_____

*"Teacher," said John, "we saw someone driving out demons in Your Name and we told him to stop because **he was not one of us**." "Do not stop him," Jesus said. "For no one who does a miracle in My Name can in the next moment say anything bad about Me, for whoever is not against us is for us." (Mark 9:38-40)*

Did only those specifically sent out by Jesus Himself receive the power to heal others?

_____

What is it that heals?

_____

*Is **anyone** among you sick? Then he must call for **the elders of the church** and they are to pray over him, anointing him with oil in the name of the Lord. And the prayer offered in faith will make the sick person well; the Lord will raise them up. If they have sinned, they will be forgiven. (James 5:14-15)*

Who should receive prayer for healing?

_____

Was the power to heal given only to the original disciples right around Jesus? Who else was it given to?

_____

_____

What is the only behavior attached to receiving healing?

_____

Who is told to have faith--the sick person, or the person who prays?

_____

What about if the sickness is attached to a sinful lifestyle?

_____

So He bent over her and rebuked the fever, and it left her. (Luke 4:39)

How did Jesus pray for healing?

_____

Was it long and complex?

_____

He took along the child's father and mother and His own companions, and entered the room where the child was. Taking the child by the hand, He said to her, "Talitha kum!" (which translated means, "Little girl, I say to you, get up!"). Immediately the girl got up and began to walk...(Mark 5:40-42)

Did Jesus "ask" for healing?

_____

Who was He commanding to leave/submit to His words?

_____

What does this tell us about His will for healing?

_____

Was He intimidated about how far gone the little girl was?

_____

A large crowd followed Him, and He healed all who were ill. (Matthew 12:15)

How many from the crowd did Jesus heal?

_____

Did He exclude any, for any reason?

_____

Were any of these people noted as special, or deserving, for any reason? What kind of people were these?

_____

*At sunset, the people brought to Jesus **all** who had various kinds of illnesses, and laying His hands on **each one**, He healed them. (Luke 4:40).*

How many did Jesus heal, that were brought to Him?

_____

Did He distinguish between any kind of people or situations?

_____

Were any conditions too hard? Did anyone deserve their illness?

_____

Did Jesus say anything or teach anything before giving them what they needed?

_____

Did anyone have to do anything first, before they could be healed? Or tell Him anything?

_____

How did He heal them?

_____

And great crowds came to Him, bringing with them the lame, the blind, the crippled, the mute, and many others, and they put them at His feet, and He healed them, so that the crowd wondered, when they saw the mute speaking, the crippled healthy, the lame walking, and the blind seeing. And they glorified the God of Israel. (Matthew 15:30-31)

Were there any cases Jesus didn't heal?

_____

Did He make anyone wait?

_____

What about those with very difficult cases-- strange, incurable, contagious, congenital conditions...?

_____

In one of the villages, Jesus met a man with an advanced case of leprosy. When the man saw Jesus, he bowed with his face to the ground, begging to be healed. "Lord," he said, "if you are willing, you can heal me and make me clean." Jesus reached out and touched him. "I am willing!" He said. "Be healed!" And instantly the leprosy disappeared. (Luke 5:12-13)

The leper knew God had the power to heal him but doubted it might be His will to do so. What did Jesus specifically declare God's will is, for healing?

_____

Did Jesus only declare that He was (theoretically) willing to heal, or did He actually do it?

_____

Did He hesitate?

_____

If you act like Jesus, how will you treat sickness?

_____

Can you be sure, when someone ill comes for prayer—or you do—that God's will is to heal?

_____

Is He powerful enough to fix anything, whether congenital, incurable, mental, emotional, demonic…?

_____

REFLECTION QUESTION:

❖ What does a life in the Holy Spirit look like?
   → *Do I want this?*

WEEK 3: THE HOLY SPIRIT

Call to Action- Say "Yes" to Knowing the Holy Spirit

Main Points-

- The Father rejoiced to give us the good gift of the Holy Spirit after Jesus died and was resurrected.
- The Holy Spirit helps us, guides us, and leads us into truth.
- Receiving the Holy Spirit specifically causes spiritual gifts to manifest in our lives.
- The purpose of spiritual gifts is to reflect the image of Jesus in the church—to supernaturally bestow His love, knowledge, edification, and equipping among His people.
- When we are truly walking by the Spirit, we bear the good fruit of the Spirit all over our lives.
- The Holy Spirit empowers us for miraculous living, including hearing and interacting with the voice of God.

Next Steps-

- ❖ *Invite the Holy Spirit* into your devotional life. Pray and ask God to reveal more of the Holy Spirit to you as you pray, worship, and read the Word. Try to tap into His flow.
- ❖ *Ask God to speak to you* through the Spirit throughout your day, as you work. The more we check in with Him, the more He usually has to say!
- ❖ *Read the Book of Acts* for a picture of who the Holy Spirit is, and how He works. Try 1 Corinthians 12-14 next.
- ❖ Sign up for the next class, *Foundations for Freedom*, to learn more about the Holy Spirit and His inner work in your life.

Key Scripture to Meditate on:

"Which of you fathers, if your son asks for a fish, will give him a snake instead? Or if he asks for an egg, will give him a scorpion? If you then, though you are evil, know how to give good gifts to your children, how much more will your Father in heaven give the Holy Spirit to those who ask him!" (Luke 11:11-13)

THE BIBLE

The Word of God
Building on the Rock

THE WORD OF GOD

A SOLID FOUNDATION

*"Everyone who **hears these words** of mine and **puts them into practice** is like a wise man who built his house on the rock. The rain came down, the streams rose, and the winds blew and beat against that house; yet it did not fall, because it had its foundation on the rock. But everyone who hears these words of mine and does not put them into practice is like a foolish man who built his house on sand. The rain came down, the streams rose, and the winds blew and beat against that house, and it fell with a great crash." (Matthew 7:24-27)*

In this passage, building your life on Jesus and His teachings is compared to what?

_____

_____

What will happen to your life if you do not build on Jesus' words?

_____

_____

What are the two components of building your house on the Rock?

_____

_____

If you build on Jesus, will you still have storms?

_____

If you build on Jesus, will your house prevail?

_____

Why is Bible study important?

_____

_____

WHAT IS THE BIBLE?

The Bible is the Inspired Word of God.

*All Scripture is **God-breathed** and is useful for teaching, rebuking, correcting and training in righteousness, so that the servant of God may be thoroughly equipped for every good work. (2 Timothy 3:16-17)*

Is the Bible made up by men?

_____

How much of the Bible is inspired by God? Are there books or stories we can cut out? Why not?

_____

_____

What kinds of things is the Bible useful for?

_____

_____

What is the point of reading your Bible?

_____

For prophecy never had its origin in the human will, but prophets, though human, spoke from God as they were carried along by the Holy Spirit. (2 Peter 1:21)

Who wrote the Bible?

_____

Who was behind this?

_____

The Bible is a Superior Source

Timothy, guard what has been entrusted to your care. Turn away from godless chatter and the opposing ideas of what is falsely called knowledge, which some have professed and thus gone astray from the faith. (1 Timothy 6:20-21).

What rivals your Bible as the source of knowledge and truth?

_____

What happens if you listen to these other sources of knowledge?

_____

"For My thoughts are not your thoughts, Nor are your ways My ways," declares the LORD. "For as the heavens are higher than the earth, so are My ways higher than your ways, And My thoughts than your thoughts. (Isaiah 55:8-9)

Do we naturally think like God?

_____

Trust in the LORD with all your heart and do not lean on your own understanding. In all your ways acknowledge Him, and He will make your paths straight. (Prov. 3:5-6)

What does God say we should do instead of relying on human wisdom?

_____

_____

What will result when we rely on God's wisdom?

_____

_____

The Bible is our guide.

Watch your life and doctrine closely. Pay close attention to yourself and to your teaching; persevere in these things, for as you do this you will ensure salvation both for yourself and for those who hear you. (1 Timothy 4:15-16)

How important is it to pay attention to what you believe?

_____

For everything that was written in the past was written to teach us, so that through the endurance taught in the Scriptures, and the encouragement they provide, we might have hope. (Romans 15:4)

A lot of the Bible is history and stories. Why are these relevant to us today?

_____

_____

The lives of many people in the Bible were very hard. How is this supposed to help you when your life is hard?

_____

_____

Now these things happened to them as an example, but they were written down for our instruction, on whom the end of the ages has come. (1 Corinthians 10:11)

Where are we supposed to get our models of right and wrong ways to live and believe?

_____

MEDITATING ON THE SCRIPTURES

Alive and Active

For the Word of God is alive and active. Sharper than any double-edged sword, it penetrates even to dividing soul and spirit, joints and marrow; it judges the thoughts and attitudes of the heart. And there is no creature hidden from His sight, but all things are open and laid bare to the eyes of Him. (Hebrews 4:12-13)

How is Scripture different from every other kind of writing?

_____

_____

What effect does allowing God's Word into your heart have?

_____

_____

If lies or sins are hiding in your life or beliefs, what effect will God's Word have on them?

_____

Continually Considering the Word

Keep this Book of the Law always on your lips; meditate on it day and night, so that you may be careful to do everything written in it. Then you will be prosperous and successful. (Joshua 1:8)

What leads to prosperity and success?

_____

What is the difference between reading and meditating?

_____

_____

Bind them on your heart always; tie them around your neck. When you walk, they will lead you; when you lie down, they will watch over you; and when you awake, they will talk with you. For the commandments are a lamp and the teachings a light, and the reproofs of discipline are the way of life. (Proverbs 6:21-23)

How does Scripture describe "meditating" on it?

_____

_____

How often are you supposed to consider what Scripture teaches?

_____

How can the words of Scripture "watch over" your life?

_____

Maturity and Wisdom

As a result, we are no longer to be children, tossed here and there by waves and carried about by every wind of doctrine, by the trickery of men, by craftiness in deceitful scheming. (Ephesians 4:14)

After we become established in the principles of Scripture, what are we able to avoid?

_____

_____

Oh, how I love your law! I meditate on it all day long. Your commands are always with me and make me wiser than my enemies. I have more insight than all my teachers, for I meditate on your statutes. I have more understanding than the elders, for I obey your precepts. I have kept my feet from every evil path so that I might obey your word. I have not departed from your laws, for you yourself have taught me. How sweet are your words to my taste, sweeter than honey to my mouth! I gain understanding from your precepts; therefore I hate every wrong path. Your word is a lamp for my feet, and a light on my path. (Psalm 119:97-105)

How wise can you become if you meditate on Scripture?

_____

If you meditate on Scripture when you have difficult life choices, how will you receive guidance?

_____

What is the result of diligent study and obedience to the Word of God?

_____

WISELY HANDLING THE SCRIPTURE

Jesus is the Center

You study the Scriptures diligently because you think that in them you have eternal life. These are the very Scriptures that testify about Me. (John 5:29)

Can reading your Bible diligently qualify you for heaven?

_____

Can getting the right theology from it qualify you for heaven?

_____

What is the real purpose of the Word?

_____

Doing what it says

Get rid of all moral filth and the evil that is so prevalent among you, and humbly accept the Word God has planted in your hearts, for it has the power to save your souls. But be doers of the Word, and not hearers only, deceiving yourselves. For anyone who listens to the Word but does not do what it says is like a man who looks intently at his face in a mirror, and after looking at himself, goes away and immediately forgets what he looks like. But the one who looks into the perfect law, the law of liberty, and perseveres in it—not forgetting what he has heard but doing it—he will be blessed in what he does. (James 1:21-25)

Does James believe in the importance of reading the Word? How can you tell?

_____

_____

Why do you think James compares the Bible to a "mirror" that shows a man what he looks like?

_____

_____

What is supposed to be the goal of reading Scripture and learning what it says?

_____

Can reading the Bible magically change you into something you are not? What is required to authentically change?

_____

What does James imply the concern would be in putting intense hours of Bible study above all other ways of relating to God?

_____

_____

Reading to "see" and connect with Jesus

*They arranged to meet Paul on a certain day, and came in even larger numbers to the place where he was staying. He witnessed to them from morning till evening, explaining about the kingdom of God, and **from the Law of Moses and from the Prophets** he tried to persuade them about Jesus. **Some were convinced** by what he said, but others would not believe.*

*They disagreed among themselves and began to leave after Paul had made this final statement: "The Holy Spirit rightly spoke through Isaiah the prophet to your fathers, saying, 'Go to this people and say, "You will keep on hearing, but will not understand; and you will keep on seeing but will not perceive; **for the heart of this people has become dull**, and with their ears they scarcely hear, and they have closed their eyes; otherwise they might see with their eyes and hear with their ears, and understand with their heart and return, and I would heal them." (Acts 28:25-27)*

Can reading the Bible (or proclaiming its truths publicly) force people into salvation?

_____

Can we assume people just need to read the Bible, and then they will believe like we do?

_____

What do people need in order to understand and believe the Bible?

_____

What must come first?

_____

Now that same day two [disciples] were going to a village called Emmaus, about seven miles from Jerusalem. They were talking with each other about everything that had happened. As they talked and discussed these things with each other, Jesus Himself came up and walked along with them; but they were kept from recognizing him. He asked them, "What are you discussing together as you walk along?..."

...He said to them, "How foolish you are, and how slow to believe all that the prophets have spoken! Did not the Messiah have to suffer these things and then enter his glory?" And beginning with Moses and all the Prophets, He explained to them what was said in all the Scriptures concerning Himself. When He was at the table with them, He took bread, gave thanks, broke it and began to give it to them.

Then their eyes were opened and they recognized Him, and He disappeared from their sight. They asked each other, "Were not our hearts burning within us while He talked with us on the road and opened the Scriptures to us?" (Luke 24:13-17, 25-32)

Two believers walking on a road were talking about Christian ideas. Jesus was there, but were they connected to Jesus as they talked about them?

_____

Are you necessarily connected to Jesus because you are having Christian conversations?

_____

Does Jesus want to be connected to your thoughts and discussions?

_____

What do you have to do, to have Him enter in?

_____

Do we automatically understand the Bible, even if we've read it and studied it at length?

_____

Who has to open our eyes and explain it to us?

_____

How are we supposed to feel when the Spirit is moving through us and helping us to interpret/apply Scripture correctly?

_____

REFLECTION QUESTION:

❖ Why do we read and study the Bible?
  → *Am I ready to believe it and obey it?*

BUILDING ON THE ROCK

THE WORLD'S FALSE FOUNDATIONS

The wrath of God is being revealed from heaven against all the godlessness and wickedness of people, who suppress the truth by their wickedness, since what may be known about God is plain to them, because God has made it plain to them. For since the creation of the world God's invisible qualities—his eternal power and divine nature—have been clearly seen, being understood from what has been made, so that people are without excuse. For although they knew God, they neither glorified him as God nor gave thanks to him, but their thinking became futile and their foolish hearts were darkened. Although they claimed to be wise, they became fools and exchanged the glory of the immortal God for images made to look like a mortal human being and birds and animals and reptiles.

Therefore God gave them over in the sinful desires of their hearts to sexual impurity for the degrading of their bodies with one another. They exchanged the truth about God for a lie, and worshiped and served created things rather than the Creator...Furthermore, just as they did not think it worthwhile to retain the knowledge of God, so God gave them over to a depraved mind, so that they do what ought not to be done. They have become filled with every kind of wickedness, evil, greed and depravity. They are full of envy, murder, strife, deceit and malice. They are gossips, slanderers, God-haters, insolent, arrogant and boastful; they invent ways of doing evil; they disobey their parents; they have no understanding, no fidelity, no love, no mercy. Although they know God's righteous decree that those who do such things deserve death, they not only continue to do these very things but also approve of those who practice them.   (Romans 1:18-32)

How is it clear there is a God, even to those who do not believe?

_____

_____

How do most people respond to the facts they have about God?

_____

_____

What kind of religion results when people refuse to respond to that truth?

_____

_____

What happens when someone turns far enough away from God?

_____

_____

How does an entire society become hateful of God?

_____

_____

Based on this passage, how do wrong ideas about God and evil practices go together?

_____

_____

Mark this: There will be terrible times in the last days. People will be lovers of themselves, lovers of money, boastful, proud, abusive, disobedient to their parents, ungrateful, unholy, without love, unforgiving, slanderous, without self-control, brutal, not lovers of the good, treacherous, rash, conceited, lovers of pleasure rather than lovers of God— having a form of godliness but denying its power. Have nothing to do with such people. (2 Timothy 3:1-5)

Do you see these things around you today?

_____

How are these things promoted?

_____

_____

_____

Pressure to conform to the world's attitudes may come in the form of an actual person, or in what other ways?

_____

_____

_____

Just became something seems good or godly, does that mean it truly is good? How do you know?

_____

_____

If you are being corrupted by worldly company, what does God ask you to do?

_____

For among them are those who worm their way into homes and captivate weak people weighed down with sins and led astray by various passions, who are swayed by all kinds of evil desires, always learning but never able to come to a knowledge of the truth. (2 Timothy 3:6-7)

Does reading or learning more always lead to truth? Why not?

_____

_____

Do you know anyone who knows more than you, or is always learning more, but is clearly deceived?

_____

What does this verse tell you about relying on your own intelligence or study habits for guidance?

_____

_____

According this passage, what is a temptation for the more dominant leaders in society? What is a weakness for those who tend to be receivers?

_____

_____

FALSE TEACHING

The time will come when people will not put up with sound doctrine. Instead, to suit their own desires, they will gather around them a great number of teachers to say what their itching ears want to hear. They will turn their ears away from the truth and turn aside to myths. (2 Timothy 4:3-4)

How can you tell you are listening to a myth made up to suit "itching ears"?

_____

_____

What sources are the "teachers" in our culture, which tell us what to believe?

_____

_____

Can these sources be trusted?

_____

See to it that no one takes you captive through hollow and deceptive philosophy, which depends on human tradition and the elemental spiritual forces of this world rather than on Christ. (Colossians 2:8)

What can you be taken captive by?

_____

Even if something sounds intelligent, if it is not based on God, what is it based on?

_____

_____

How does the Bible describe these philosophies which are not based on Christ?

_____

_____

*So also we, while we were children, were held in bondage **under the basic principles of the world**...Formerly, when you did not know God, you were slaves to those who by nature are not gods. But now that you know God--or rather are known by God-- how is it that you are turning back to those weak and miserable forces? Do you wish to be enslaved by them all over again? (Galatians 4:3, 8-9)*

"Basic principles of the world" are not complex philosophies but popular ideas and ways of life. Are there any "basic principles" of the world around you, which people say you should believe while God says you should feel differently?

_____

_____

Where do these ideas lead?

_____

When you follow Christ, He asks you to reject these principles. But what is the temptation?

_____

_____

You gladly put up with fools since you are so wise! In fact, you even put up with anyone who enslaves you or exploits you, or takes advantage of you, or puts on airs or slaps you in the face. (2 Corinthians 11:9-20)

According to this verse, those who teach false doctrines do not only seduce you, what else do they do to keep you from the truth?

_____

_____

From the least to the greatest, all are greedy for gain; prophets and priests alike, all practice deceit. They dress the wound of my people as though it were not serious. 'Peace, peace,' they say, when there is no peace. Are they ashamed of their detestable conduct? No, they have no shame at all; they do not even know how to blush. So they will fall among the fallen; they will be brought down when I punish them. (Jeremiah 6:13)

What is the end result of following the lies of the false prophets of your generation?

_____

_____

_____

This verse indicates that your thoughts and ideas need to "obey" Christ, just like your behavior. Which do you think the bigger war is?

_____

Why?

_____

_____

What is the ultimate standard of Truth by which you can judge all arguments?

_____

COMMON TRAPS

*But I am afraid that as the serpent deceived Eve by his cunning, your thoughts will be led astray from a sincere and pure devotion to Christ. For if someone comes and proclaims another Jesus than the one we proclaimed, or if you receive a different spirit from the one you received, or if you accept a **different gospel** from the one you accepted, you put up with it readily enough. (2 Corinthians 11:3-4)*

What are the three situations that Paul links to being the same kind of deception that befell Adam and Eve?

_____

_____

If the only way to heaven is through Jesus' love for us, and His death on the Cross, what is the mark of a "different gospel"?

_____

_____

Therefore do not let anyone judge you by what you eat or drink, or with regard to a religious festival, a New Moon celebration, or a Sabbath day. These are a shadow of the things that were to come; the reality, however, is found in Christ.

What kinds of things does Paul say not to get caught up in?

_____

In what ways have you seen that these are popular fascinations today?

_____

_____

_____

Why aren't we to get caught up in these things?

_____

_____

_____

Do not let anyone who delights in false humility and the worship of angels disqualify you. Such a person also goes into great detail about what they have seen; they are puffed up with idle notions by their unspiritual mind. They have lost connection with the Head, from whom the whole body, supported and held together by its ligaments and sinews, grows as God causes it to grow (Colossians 2:18-19)

What kinds of things does Paul say not to get caught up in here?

_____

_____

What does the Scripture say results from being continually transfixed by spiritual experiences and personal revelations?

_____

_____

If you have died with Christ to the spiritual forces of the world, why, as though you still belonged to the world, do you submit to its regulations: "Do not handle, do not taste, do not touch!"? These will all perish with use because they are based on human commands and teachings. Such restrictions indeed have an appearance of wisdom, with their self-prescribed worship, their false humility, and their harsh treatment of the body; but they are of no value against the indulgence of the flesh. (Colossians 2:20-23)

Does avoiding certain foods, chemicals, or lifestyle practices make you more spiritual?

_____

Why not-- What is the origin of these teachings?

_____

_____

What does this passage call restrictive lifestyles?

_____

_____

Why doesn't punishing yourself, imposing rigid regulations on yourself, or subjecting your body to "harsh treatment" work?

_____

_____

_____

_____

Timothy, guard what has been entrusted to your care. Turn away from godless chatter and the opposing ideas of what is falsely called knowledge, which some have professed and thus gone astray from the faith." (1 Timothy 6:20-21).

False gospels and worldly teaching can lead people to think they have found a secret key of "knowledge" about something—especially if people are not commonly teaching it. What are we supposed to do when we run into them?

_____

_____

"Godless chatter" is meaningless talk about worldly things. It may seem harmless, but where does it lead?

_____

_____

We destroy arguments and every lofty opinion raised against the knowledge of God, and take every thought captive to obey Christ. (2 Corinthians 10:5)

What is our job when we run into thoughts which go against God and His perspective?

_____

_____

How much attention and reflection will this require? Is this something we can do passively?

_____

_____

REFLECTION QUESTIONS:

- ❖ What kinds of worldly philosophies or "different gospels" are around me right now?
- ❖ Are there practical things I should do to escape the influence and pressure around me to believe them?

WEEK 4: THE BIBLE

Call to Action- Say "Yes" to Getting into the Word of God

Main Points-

- The Bible is inspired by God and reliable in everything it says.
- God gave us the written Word to guide us, above other sources of knowledge or what we ourselves think.
- He asks us to meditate on the truth and do what it says, as opposed to merely reading it and working through theological doctrine.
- The goal of all Bible study is for us to know Jesus more and walk with Him better.
- The world will reject us as foolish for standing on revealed knowledge from God rather than on their authorities.
- The Word can be twisted to say what people or teachers want it to say. The New Testament has many instructions about different kinds of distortions, and emphasizes the simple gospel.

Next Steps-

- ❖ *Get a study Bible* with good notes and cross-references to help you understand the Word when you read it—the *Spirit-Filled Life Bible*, the *Fire Bible*, and the *NIV Study Bible* are good options.
- ❖ Try *watching a gospel or book of the Bible* on video, which can bring out different aspects of the text. *The Bible* mini-series on DVD is one suggestion.
- ❖ Try a resource such as *The Story* which emphasizes the main themes of the entire Bible, and the big picture. Or try a visual organizer of what's in the Bible such as *Rose's Charts, Maps, and Timelines*.
- ❖ *Sign up for a Bible class* at Radiant to learn more about the Word and the reliability of the Scripture.

Key Scripture to Meditate on:

Your Word is a lamp unto my feet, and a light unto my path. (Psalm 119:105)

THE CHURCH

A Holy Gathering
The Church's Mission

A Holy Gathering

GOD'S HEART FOR CHURCH

Meeting together

Let us not neglect meeting together, as some have made a habit, but let us encourage one another, and all the more as you see the Day approaching. *—Hebrews 10:25*

Should we be gathering together? Regularly?

_____

What is the purpose of the gathering?

_____

How long should gathering for church continue?

_____

Gathering in agreement

I tell you truly that if two of you on the earth agree about anything you ask for, it will be done for you by My Father in heaven. For where two or three gather together in My name, there am I with them. *—Matthew 18:19-20*

Is Jesus present when we gather?

_____

What is the simplest definition of "church" presented here?

_____

_____

Christians meet in separate buildings, but who/what unites us?

_____

According to this Scripture, why is uniting powerful?

_____

_____

Spiritual Family

Looking at those seated in a circle around Him, He said, "Here are My mother and My brothers! For whoever does the will of God is My brother and sister and mother."
—Mark 3:34-35

What did this first "church" meeting look like?

_____

How does Jesus rename the believers around Him?

_____

Does Jesus have family, according to this verse? Who are they?

_____

_____

Why does Jesus describe the gathering this way-- What kind of love and unity does a family ideally have?

_____

_____

→   The church is a holy gathering of people around Him. They behold Him, listen to Him, and pray for His will, together—so that they are bound in a special kind of love and unity while on earth, which foreshadows heaven.

THE CORPORATE BODY

Behold, the LORD has proclaimed to the ends of the earth, "Say to Daughter Zion: See, your Savior comes! Look, His reward is with Him, and His recompense goes before Him." And they will be called a Holy People, the Redeemed of the LORD; and you will be called 'Sought Out, A City Not Forsaken.' " —Isaiah 62:11-12

120

How does God address Zion, His saved people?

_____

What words here show that God's heart's desire is a *corporate* gathering before Him?

_____

_____

Is "church", the corporate gathering, a new, New Testament concept?

_____

Is the corporate gathering before Him temporary or eternal? Will the church disappear in the eternal age?

_____

Jesus died for "the church"

...Christ is the head of the church, His body, of which He is the Savior...–Eph. 5:23

What is Christ currently the chief executive of?

_____

How is the church described, relative to Jesus? Why does He use this analogy?

_____

_____

The Church is His Body (still) on earth.

From Him the whole Body is fitted and held together by every supporting ligament. And as each individual part does its work, the Body grows and builds itself up in love. –Ephesians 4:16

Does the power in Christianity lie in any one person?

_____

Do you have value in the Body? Why?

_____

_____

What allows us to be knit together, even though we are all different?

_____

_____

For the body does not consist of one part, but of many... if the ear should say, "Because I am not an eye, I do not belong to the body," that would not make it any less a part of the body. If the whole body were an eye, where would the sense of hearing be? ...In fact, God has arranged the members of the body, every one of them, according to His design...

As it is, there are many parts, but one body. The eye cannot say to the hand, "I do not need you." Nor can the head say to the feet, "I do not need you." On the contrary, the parts of the body that seem to be weaker are indispensable, and the parts we consider less honorable, we treat with greater honor... God has composed the body and has given greater honor to the parts that lacked it, so that there should be no division in the body, but that its members should have mutual concern for one another. —1 Corinthians 12:14-25

Is Christianity supposed to be just individuals pursuing God?

_____

Is there supposed to be an institutional or organizational part to the Body of Christ on the earth? How can you tell?

_____

_____

Who has designed Christianity to be corporate-- and the parts of the Body to be how they are?

_____

Are there things you can't do, or don't like to do? How does a corporate Body help that?

_____

_____

Why shouldn't we esteem our own talents, trying hard to get them seen or heard in the Body?

_____

_____

How should we treat faithful members who cannot contribute much?

_____

The Body is for the completion of the tasks God has given us. How does division or jealousy affect our success at that?

_____

_____

Peace and unity among members

For He Himself is our peace, who has made the two one and has torn down the dividing wall of hostility... He did this to create in Himself one new man out of the two, thus making peace and reconciling both of them to God in one body through the Cross, by which He extinguished their hostility...

How did the Cross tear down the "dividing walls of hostility" which separate different kinds of people?

_____

_____

_____

Therefore you are no longer strangers and foreigners, but fellow citizens with the saints and members of God's household, built on the foundation of the apostles and prophets, with Christ Jesus Himself as the cornerstone. In Him the whole building is fitted together and grows into a holy temple in the Lord. And in Him you too are being built together into a dwelling place for God in His Spirit. -Ephesians 2:14-22

Why can we have peace in Him?

_____

_____

What causes us to be able to host God's presence together?

_____

→ Christianity is a worldwide family committed to God together. We are a holy gathering. We build and care better as a team.

GATHERING FOR WORSHIP

Joy and Praise

Praise God in His sanctuary! Praise Him in His mighty heavens. Praise Him for His mighty acts; praise Him for His excellent greatness. Praise Him with the sound of the horn; praise Him with the harp and lyre. Praise Him with tambourine and dancing; praise Him with strings and flute. Praise Him with clashing cymbals; praise Him with resounding cymbals. Let everything that has breath praise the LORD! --Psalm 150

Clap your hands, all you peoples; shout unto God with a voice of triumph. —Psalm 47:1

When we come to God in "His sanctuary," what are we to do?

_____

What are we praising Him for? What should be the focus of our messages and thankfulness?

_____

_____

Is it ok to clap in church, have loud instruments, or a shout?

_____

How engaged are we to be? Does He imagine us just doing our duty and leaving, or sitting in the back?

_____

Is there physical engagement during worship, or just your own mind?

_____

Holiness

Who may ascend the hill of the LORD? Who may stand in His holy place? He who has clean hands and a pure heart... -Psalm 24:3-4

How does God desire us to come to church?

_____

Can He see how our thoughts and deeds have been during the week?

_____

Reconciliation

So if you are offering your gift at the altar and there remember that your brother has something against you, leave your gift there before the altar. First go and be reconciled to your brother; then come and offer your gift. –Matthew 5:23-24

Should we come to church without examining ourselves?

_____

What particular thing seems to be on God's mind as we worship Him in church?

_____

Therefore I desire men in every place to pray, lifting up holy hands, apart from anger and dissension. -Titus 1:8

When we lift our hands or pray, what is God hoping we have put aside?

_____

They devoted themselves to the apostles' teaching, and to the fellowship, to the breaking of bread, and to prayer. –Acts 2:42

What did the church services of Jesus' first followers include?

_____

How committed to community were they?

_____

Do these first services sound like formal routines, a liturgy, or something else?

_____

_____

Teaching

Early in the morning, He [Jesus] went back into the temple courts. All the people came to Him, and He sat down to teach them. —John 8:3

Jesus was teaching at the Temple every day... —Luke 19:39

When and where did Jesus hold His first church services?

_____

What characterized those services?

_____

Every Sabbath he [Paul] reasoned in the synagogue, trying to persuade Jews and Greeks alike. —Acts 18:4

Paul went into the synagogue and spoke boldly there for three months, arguing persuasively about the Kingdom of God. —Acts 19:8

What can we infer Paul's weekly service was like, according to these verses?

_____

_____

Prayer

*Jesus entered the temple courts and began to drive out those who were selling there. He declared to them, "It is written: '**My house** will be a house of prayer,' but you have made it a den of robbers.." —Luke 19:45-46*

How did Jesus describe the vision for His house, the building which was supposed to be devoted to worshipping Him?

_____

Evangelism

*So the master told his servant, "Go out to the highways and the hedges and compel them to come in, so that **my house** will be full." —Luke 14:23*

Should we have evangelistic services?

_____

Healing and Ministry

Is any one of you sick? He should call the elders of the church to pray over him and anoint him with oil in the name of the Lord. —James 5:14

Should the church pray for the sick?

_____

When you come together, each of you has a hymn, or a word of instruction, a revelation, a tongue, or an interpretation. Let all things be done so that the church is edified. -1 Corinthians 14:26

Does God want all people to be ministers, or just the one speaking on Sunday?

_____

What kinds of things could be evident among the Body during a typical service?

_____

_____

What should be the point of all things shared as a community on Sundays?

_____

What does emphasizing the need to edify the church, or build each other up, imply? –i.e. about our experiences in the world the rest of the week?

_____

_____

Giving and Charity

Bring the full tithe into the storehouse so that there may be food in My house. Test Me in this," says the LORD of Hosts. "See if I will not open the windows of heaven and pour out for you blessing without measure." -Malachi 3:10

According to this verse, why does God say to tithe?

_____

What constitutes "food"? What kinds of things do tithes allow churches to do?

_____

_____

If churches and ministries did not have these resources, how would that set back our culture?

_____

_____

How can you be sure God will provide for you, if you give in this way?

_____

_____

BEING A HEALTHY MEMBER

*Surely you heard of Him and were taught in Him— in keeping with the truth that is in Jesus— **to put off your former way of life, your old self**, which is being corrupted by its deceitful desires; and to be renewed in the spirit of your minds; **and to put on the new self**, created to be like God in true righteousness and holiness.*

*Therefore **each of you** must put off falsehood and speak truthfully to his neighbor, for **we are all members of one body**. Be angry, yet do not sin. Do not let the sun set upon your anger, and do not give the devil a foothold. He who has been stealing must steal no longer, but must work, doing good with his own hands, that he may have something to share with the one in need. Let no unwholesome talk come out of your mouths, but only what is helpful for building up the one in need and bringing grace to those who listen...Get rid of all bitterness, rage and anger, outcry and slander, along with every form of malice. Be kind and tenderhearted to **one another**, forgiving **each other** just as in Christ God forgave you. —Ephesians 4:21-32*

Is it easy to become your "new self?" To "renew" your mind?

_____

Name a few things that need to end, as healthy members of the Body.

_____

_____

Why won't praying and reading your Bible, in isolation, achieve these?

_____

_____

Having good models

Join one another in following my example, brothers, and carefully observe those who walk according to the pattern we set for you. -Philippians 3:17

Follow me, as I follow Christ. —1 Corinthians 11:1

Paul says we need models. Where can we find them?

_____

Having good leaders

An overseer must be above reproach, the husband of but one wife, temperate, self-controlled, respectable, hospitable, able to teach, not dependent on wine, not violent but gentle, peaceable, and free of the love of money. An overseer must manage his own household well and keep his children under control, with complete dignity. For if someone does not know how to manage his own household, how can he care for the church of God? —1 Timothy 3:1-5

Would you appreciate a leader who had the qualifications above?

_____

Why would having healthy family relationships be a good qualification for a mentor or church leader?

_____

_____

Why should the church encourage strong, healthy families as part of its mission?

_____

_____

Good friends and support.

A friend loves at all times, and a brother is born for a time of adversity. *—Prov. 17:7*

Scripture says we need friends. Where can we find them?

_____

How can we be a good friend to our brothers and sisters in church?

_____

I am a companion of all who fear you, of those who keep your commandments. *—Psalm 119:63*

To be healthy, who should be our friends?

_____

If you are dating, who should you be partnering yourself with?

_____

Why?

_____

130

Do you believe you can find good friends for you or your family at church? If not, consider why not and ask Jesus about these reasons.

_____

_____

> → Church is a place we can care for others and be cared for. Relationships, service roles, and many aspects of community shape us into the people we need to be. Worshipping God together changes our hearts, as we engage with holiness and passion.

REFLECTION QUESTION:

❖ Why do we go to church?
> → *Is anything holding me back from being in community, or an engaged part of the Body of Christ?*

THE CHURCH'S MISSION

PARTNERING WITH GOD

*His purpose was that now, **through the church**, the manifold wisdom of God should be made known to the rulers and authorities in the heavenly realms, according to the eternal purpose that he accomplished in Christ Jesus our Lord. Then the End will come when He hands over the kingdom to God the Father... For He must reign until He has put all His enemies under His feet... For God has put everything in subjection under His feet. —1 Corinthians 15:24-27*

Is God using the church?

_____

Did He choose to use the church intentionally? When did He decide this?

_____

_____

What is He making known, and to whom?

_____

_____

Who makes it possible for the church to be His change agent in this way?

_____

For what period of time are we the hands and feet of Jesus?

_____

_____

How does Scripture characterize this time period? What are we helping Jesus to accomplish?

_____

_____

And he has made known to us the mystery of his will, according to his good pleasure, which he purposed in Christ as a plan for the fullness of time, to bring all things in heaven and on earth together in Christ.   —Ephesians 1:9-10

What was God's heart desire, from the beginning of time?

_____

_____

When was the world let in on this secret?

_____

Is earth in perfect alignment with heaven, where His will is always done?

_____

Who is partnering with Him to help make this happen?

_____

Will God get what He is looking for?

_____

I tell you that you are Peter, and on this rock I will build My church, and the gates of hell will not prevail [win over, gain power] against it.   —Matthew 16:18

What did Jesus—formerly a carpenter—want to build?

_____

Whose church is it?

_____

Is the church victorious now?

_____

Will we be victorious in the future?

_____

The kingdom of heaven is like a mustard seed that a man planted in his field. Although it is the smallest of all seeds, yet it grows into the largest of garden plants

and becomes a tree so that the birds of the air come and nest in its branches.
–Matthew 13:31-33

All the birds of the air took shelter in its branches...and all the great nations lived in its shade. –Ezekiel 31:6

Does the church need strength and size in order to succeed?

_____

What kind of environment attracts birds to come and nest?

_____

_____

What ways does the church offer this to the world?

_____

_____

The disciples asked Him, "How should we pray?" Jesus answered, "Our Father, who is in heaven, holy is your name. Your Kingdom Come [and] Your will be done on earth, as it is in heaven..." –Matthew 6:9-10

According to Jesus, what should the church be praying for?

_____

_____

What happens if we neglect this?

_____

_____

How can the church also be an answer to this kind of prayer?

_____

_____

When this [deliverance] became known to the Jews and Greeks living in Ephesus, they were all seized with fear, and the name of the Lord Jesus was held in high honor. Many of those who believed now came forward, confessing and disclosing their deeds. A number who had practiced sorcery brought their scrolls together and burned them publicly. When they calculated the value of the scrolls, the total came to fifty thousand drachmas [several million dollars, NLT]. In this way the word of the Lord spread widely and grew in power. —Acts 19:17-20

How did revival change the way this society felt about the name of Jesus?

_____

_____

What did honoring God cause people to do?

_____

_____

Was their repentance deep or superficial?

_____

Did they care about their wealth and sources of success?

_____

What did corporate repentance on this scale then cause?

_____

_____

→ Transformed lives means transformed communities expressing themselves on the earth. This is God's will for his church, and what we're partnering with Him in.

LOVING EACH OTHER

With one accord they continued to meet daily in the temple courts and to break bread from house to house, sharing their meals with gladness and sincerity of heart, praising God and enjoying the favor of all the people. And the Lord added to their number daily those who were being saved. Acts 2:46-47

How do you feel about this as a description of church?

_____

Were the early believers in unity when they met?

_____

How can you tell they were glad and joyful?

_____

_____

Practically speaking, what would you need to do on a Sunday meeting to feel this kind of joy and gladness?

_____

_____

Could you do that? If not, why not?

_____

_____

What two things resulted from this comradery?

_____

_____

Love the brotherhood of believers. -1 Peter 2:17

How are we to feel about church, other believers?

_____

How does God describe our fellow believers, locally and across the globe?

_____

If there are ways you have criticized the church, believers, or Christianity, take a moment now to confess those and give any reasons to Jesus.

_____

_____

Christ loved the church and gave Himself up for her to make her holy, cleansing her by the washing with water through the Word, to present her to Himself as a radiant church, without stain or wrinkle or blemish, but holy and blameless. (Eph. 5:24-27)

How does Jesus feel about the church?

_____

Is His love strong? Does it have purpose?

_____

What did His death accomplish, for the church?

_____

_____

How does loving each other well help fulfill this Scripture?

_____

_____

LEADERSHIP

"Didn't you know I'd be in my Father's house?" –Luke 2:49

What did Jesus call the temple?

_____

Why did He call it this? What is the main function of a house?

_____

_____

Is the church a house of our own making? Who is really in charge?

_____

And it was He who gave some to be apostles, some to be prophets, some to be evangelists, and some to be pastors and teachers, to equip the saints for works of ministry, to build up the Body of Christ.   –Ephesians 4:11-12

Who decided how the church should be organized?

_____

What five offices/roles does Paul outline here, as foundational for church?

_____

_____

What is the purpose of the saints meeting under godly leadership?

_____

_____

How should the Body feel under their leaders? What should be the result?

_____

_____

Keep watch over yourselves and the entire flock of which the Holy Spirit has made you overseers. Be shepherds of the church of God, which He purchased with His own blood. —Acts 20:28

What words/phrases does Paul use to describe godly leadership of the church?

_____

_____

According to this verse, why does God care so much about pastors being good shepherds?

_____

_____

Young men, in the same way, submit yourselves to your elders. —1 Peter 5:5

What is the purpose of eldership?

In the same way, deacons are to be worthy of respect, sincere, not indulging in much wine, and not pursuing dishonest gain. They must keep hold of the deep truths of the faith with a clear conscience. They must first be tested; and then if there is nothing against them, let them serve as deacons. —1 Timothy 3:8-10

There are many instructions for church leaders in Paul's epistles. Why?

_____

_____

Based on this verse, what do you think the leadership "test" here entails?

_____

_____

Why would God want His overseers to be tested in this way?

_____

_____

I am reminded of your sincere faith, which first dwelt in your grandmother Lois and your mother Eunice, and I am convinced is in you as well. —1 Timothy 1:5

How did Timothy's leadership career actually begin?

_____

_____

How is having strong, healthy families in your church important to having a strong, healthy church?

_____

_____

CARE IN THE COMMUNITY

In those days when the disciples were increasing in number, the Greek-speaking Jews among them began to grumble against the Hebrew-speaking Jews because their widows were being overlooked in the daily distribution of food... "Therefore, brothers, select from among you seven men confirmed to be full of the Spirit and wisdom. We will appoint this responsibility to them." -Acts 6:3

Should the church take care of the less fortunate among them?

_____

Should the church have structure and organization?

_____

When did the need for more structure and organization become necessary?

_____

What features do you notice in how this church solved their ministry and leadership situation?

_____

_____

Each one should give what he has decided in his heart to give, not out of regret or compulsion. For God loves a cheerful giver. – 2 Corinthians 9:7

What regulates whether we should give, or how much?

_____

Why then would God want His people to give, or care about that?

_____

_____

Have you ever given non-cheerfully or "under compulsion"? Why doesn't God want us to tithe or give charitably this way?

_____

_____

Think about a person or situation that you gave to, that made a difference in their lives and also blessed you. How could you enlarge this area of grace, to see that a little more often?

_____

_____

I urge that petitions, prayers, intercessions, and thanksgiving be offered for everyone—for rulers and all those in authority-- so that we may lead tranquil and quiet lives in all godliness and dignity. This is good and pleasing in the sight of God our Savior... --1 Timothy 2:1-3

How does God picture His people living their daily lives, as a corporate Body dwelling on earth?

_____

_____

How can we dwell in more tranquility and dignity, as followers of Jesus?

_____

_____

If it is possible, as much as it depends on you, live peaceably with all men. --Romans 12:18

What is important to God, as a witness of Him and your church?

_____

How would this simple quality bless a community?

_____

_____

REFLECTION QUESTION:

❖ Why did God want church? What did He intend it to be?
→ *What does this mean to me, as I take part in it?*

WEEK 5: THE CHURCH

Call to Action- Say "Yes" to Engaging in the Community and Becoming a Healthy
Member of His Body

Main Points-

- God desires His people to meet regularly in prayer and holiness.
- He died for the corporate Body, and gathering in church in His name and in His will reflects that.
- The New Testament model of church includes praise and worship, fellowship, teaching, prayer, ministry, giving, and spiritual gifts operating.
- A life-giving community reaches out and ministers to those who are in. We are both givers and receivers of care.
- We grow in community. A healthy church provides good models, leaders, and friends who support our growth in Jesus.

Next Steps-

- ❖ *Join a team* at Radiant where you can contribute and grow.
- ❖ *Join a small group* at Radiant for fellowship, connection, edification.
- ❖ Make an effort to sow into your *godly relationships* and attend each other's Bible studies, church events, etc. to build each other up.
- ❖ Set aside a few times per month to participate in corporate opportunities like *prayer meetings, service days, and churchwide celebrations.*

Key Scripture to Meditate on:

Now you are the Body of Christ, and each one of you is a member of it. (1 Corinthians 12:27)

THE GREAT COMMISSION

Partners in the Gospel
Making a Difference

Partners in the Gospel

JESUS CAME TO SAVE THE LOST

For the Son of Man has come to seek and to save that which was lost. (Luke 19:10)

What was Jesus' purpose in coming to earth?

_____

What Being "Lost" Means

*Cain said to his brother Abel, "Let us go out to the field." And while they were in the field, Cain rose up against his brother Abel and killed him. And the LORD said to Cain, "Where is your brother Abel?" "I do not know!" he answered. "Am I my brother's keeper?" "What have you done?" replied the LORD. "The voice of your brother's blood cries out to Me from the ground. Now you are **cursed** and **banished** from the ground, which has opened its mouth to receive your brother's blood from your hand. When you till the ground, it will no longer yield its produce to you. **You will be a fugitive and a wanderer on the earth**."*

*But Cain said to the LORD, "My punishment is greater than I can bear. Behold, this day You have driven me from the face of the earth, and **from Your face I will be hidden**; I will be a fugitive and a wanderer on the earth, and whoever finds me will kill me." So Cain **went out from the presence of the LORD** and settled in the land of Nod, east of Eden... Then Cain built a city... (Genesis 4:8-17)*

Cain was the first "lost" person. What was Cain's punishment for killing his brother?

_____

_____

What kinds of emotions did this cause Cain?

_____

How was Cain's relationship with God characterized from this point on?

_____

_____

What kinds of emotions and experiences would characterize the city of people that Cain led?

_____

What Happens to the Lost

There was a rich man who was clothed in purple and fine linen and who feasted sumptuously every day. And at his gate was laid a poor man named Lazarus, covered with sores, who desired to be fed with what fell from the rich man's table. Moreover, even the dogs came and licked his sores. The poor man died and was carried by the angels to Abraham's side. The rich man also died and was buried, and in Hades [hell], being in torment, he lifted up his eyes and saw Abraham far off and Lazarus at his side. And he called out, 'Father Abraham, have mercy on me, and send Lazarus to dip the end of his finger in water and cool my tongue, for I am in anguish in this flame.'

But Abraham said, 'Child, remember that you in your lifetime received your good things, and Lazarus in like manner bad things; but now he is comforted here, and you are in anguish. And besides all this, between us and you a great chasm has been fixed, in order that those who would pass from here to you may not be able, and none may cross from there to us.' And the rich man said, 'Then I beg you, father, to send him to my father's house— for I have five brothers—so that he may warn them, lest they also come into this place of torment...' (Luke 16:19-28)

How does the Bible describe hell?

_____

_____

Can people get out of it once they are there?

_____

After realizing his own eternal situation, what does the man in hell beg Abraham to do?

_____

What is the only thing that can save his family?

_____

How can we be the hero in this story?

_____

148

Why People are Lost

The god of this world has blinded the minds of the unbelievers, to keep them from seeing the light of the gospel of the glory of Christ, who is the image of God... For God, who said, "Let light shine out of darkness," made his light shine in our hearts. (2 Corinthians 4:4, 6)

What is the spiritual condition of the world, without the gospel?

_____

Who is responsible for consigning people to hell?

_____

What is God's response to that?

_____

In light of eternity in heaven or hell, does anything else compare in significance?

_____

What do you think is the main thing on God's mind every day?

_____

Jesus' Saving Heart

So He told them this parable: "What man of you, having a hundred sheep, if he has lost one of them, does not leave the ninety-nine in the open country, and go after the one that is lost, until he finds it? And when he has found it, he lays it on his shoulders, rejoicing. And when he comes home, he calls together his friends and his neighbors, saying to them, 'Rejoice with me, for I have found my sheep that was lost.' Just so, I tell you, there will be more joy in heaven over one sinner who repents than over ninety-nine righteous persons who need no repentance." (Luke 15:3-7)

How does a real shepherd care for his sheep-- what is his main job?

_____

What is He willing to do/risk to rescue one?

_____

What happens in heaven when you rescue someone?

_____

What does God calling them "lost" imply about their belonging?

_____

Jesus went throughout all the cities and villages, teaching in their synagogues and proclaiming the gospel of the kingdom and healing every disease and every affliction. When He saw the crowds, He had compassion for them, because they were harassed and helpless, like sheep without a shepherd. (Matthew 9:35-36).

Did Jesus blame people for being lost? Judge them?

_____

Why not? What was Jesus' attitude?

_____

It is not the healthy who need a doctor, but the sick. (Mark 2:17).

Why does Jesus liken those who are lost to those who are sick?

_____

Thinking about the Lost like Him.

I am the Good Shepherd. The good shepherd lays his life down for the sheep. (John 10:11)

If you are like Jesus, what will you do for people?

_____

What might this look like for you, in everyday life?

_____

_____

OUR COMMISSION TO EVANGELIZE

Our Role as Messengers

*While walking by the Sea of Galilee, [Jesus] saw two brothers, Simon who is called Peter and Andrew his brother, casting a net into the sea, for they were fishermen. And He said to them, "Follow me, and I will make you **fishers of men**. (Mat. 4:18-19)*

What did Jesus mean by calling His disciples "fishers of men"? What was Jesus going to train them to do?

_____

This was Jesus' very first command to His followers. Does He want us to wait until we've done a lot of amazing things before we share our faith?

_____

*Since, then, we know what it is to fear the Lord, we try to **persuade others**...All this is from God, who reconciled us to himself through Christ and **gave us the ministry of reconciliation**: that God was reconciling the world to himself in Christ, not counting people's sins against them. And **He has committed to us** the message of reconciliation. We are therefore Christ's **ambassadors**, as though God were making his **appeal** through us. We **implore** you on Christ's behalf: Be reconciled to God. (2 Corinthians 5:11, 18-20)*

What ministry has God given to every believer?

_____

What are the two components to "reconciliation"?

_____

_____

Why do you think Paul compares this to being an "ambassador"?

_____

_____

What kind of emotion does Paul display here, towards the lost?

_____

What kind of attitude does the Father have about reaching His lost children?

_____

The Great Commission

*And Jesus came and said to them, "All authority in heaven and on earth has been given to me. **Go therefore and make disciples of all nations**, baptizing them in the name of the Father and of the Son and of the Holy Spirit, teaching them to observe all that I have commanded you. And behold, I am with you always, to the end of the age. (Matthew 28:18-20)*

This is Jesus' last command to His followers. Did Jesus ask them to be nice people and go to church?

_____

What did He send them out to do?

_____

_____

How far were they supposed to go?

_____

How long were they supposed to preach?

_____

How much authority was available to get their job done?

_____

Many things must be done to "disciple the nations," but what should every true Christian activity come back to?

_____

Witnesses to the Whole World

*But you will receive power when the Holy Spirit has come upon you, and you will be My **witnesses** in Jerusalem and in all Judea and Samaria, and to the ends of the earth." (Acts 1:8)*

What is a witness? What does a witness promise to tell?

_____

_____

Was the power of the Holy Spirit given for just personal growth?

_____

*And they sang a new song, saying, 'Worthy are you to take the scroll and to open its seals, for you were slain, and by your blood **you ransomed people for God from every tribe and language and people and nation**.' (Revelation 5:9)*

Jesus died on the Cross to purchase which people?

_____

Has "every tribe and language and people and nation" been reached yet?

_____

What does this mean about our mission?

_____

*For everyone who calls on the name of the Lord will be saved. But how will they call on Him in whom they have not believed? And how are they to believe in Him of whom they have never heard? How are they to hear without someone preaching? And how are they to preach **unless they are sent**? As it is written, "How beautiful are the **feet** of those who preach the good news!" (Romans 10:13-15)*

How many people are required to reach an entire globe, for Christ?

_____

Why are the "feet" of missionaries called "beautiful"?

_____

If you do not evangelize, who are some people around you who would be at risk of dying without hearing the truth?

_____

_____

An Optimistic Enterprise

Then He said to his disciples, "The harvest is plentiful, but the laborers are few; therefore pray earnestly to the Lord of the Harvest to send out laborers into His harvest." (Matthew 9:37-38)

For what reason did Jesus say His followers should pray for laborers?

_____

In what ways can we help answer this prayer?

_____

_____

Truly, truly, I say to you, whoever believes in me will also do the works that I do; and greater works than these will he do, because I am going to the Father. (John 14:12)

Does Jesus expect all His followers to evangelize?

_____

Does Jesus give us reason to be *hopeful* or *doubtful* about our evangelism?

_____

STANDING STRONG

Unashamed of the Gospel

Therefore do not be ashamed of the testimony about our Lord, nor of me his prisoner, but share in suffering for the gospel by the power of God, who saved us and called us to a holy calling. (2 Timothy 1:9)

Is it normal to face pressure and attack for evangelizing?

_____

How does God want you to feel in response?

_____

154

For I am not ashamed of the gospel, for it is the power of God for salvation to everyone who believes, to the Jew first and also to the Greek. (Romans 1:16)

If you are not ashamed of the gospel, how will you witness to others?

_____

Does Jesus want you to evangelize only privately or to your friends?

_____

What kinds of things show that Christians are ashamed of the truth?

_____

Therefore everyone who confesses Me before men, I will also confess him before My Father in heaven. But whoever denies Me before men, I will also deny him before My Father in heaven…. Matthew 6:32-33

What will we do, if we authentically love Jesus?

_____

How does He reward us for this risk on earth?

_____

Enduring Hardship

*You therefore must **endure hardness** as a **good soldier** of Jesus Christ. No one engaged in warfare entangles himself with the affairs of this life, that he may please him who enlisted him as a soldier…Pray also for me, that whenever I speak, words may be given me so that I will **fearlessly** make known the mystery of the gospel, for which I am an **ambassador** in chains that I may declare it **boldly**, as I ought to speak. (Ephesians 6:19-20)*

What kind of attitude do you need, to share the gospel?

_____

_____

What will happen if you get distracted by the things of the world?

_____

Should we hide our witness? How ought we to speak?

_____

_____

*"When they **persecute** you in one town, flee to the next..." (Matthew 5:23)*

*"And you will be **hated** by all for my name's sake. But the one who endures to the end will be saved." (Matthew 5:22)*

Why is it hard to be an evangelist?

_____

How can you counteract this, in a healthy way?

_____

_____

What will your reward be, for persevering for His sake?

_____

Discharging Your Duty

As you enter the house, greet it. And if the house is worthy, let your peace come upon it, but if it is not worthy, let your peace return to you. And if anyone will not receive you or listen to your words, shake off the dust from your feet when you leave that house or town. Truly, I say to you, it will be more bearable on the day of judgment for the land of Sodom and Gomorrah than for that town. (Matthew 10: 5-15)

Jesus says our job is to preach the truth. Which two ways will people respond to this?

_____

_____

Are you supposed to let it bother you when people reject you? Or reject the gospel?

_____

Should you respond with more force? Or fire and brimstone? What emotion does Jesus say should be dominant at all times?

_____

What are you responsible for, and what are your hearers responsible for?

_____

_____

REFLECTION QUESTION:

❖ Why does Jesus need me to share my faith?
  → *Am I stirred by that? What holds me back?*

Making a Difference

JOINING THE MISSION

Then Jesus came to them and said, "All authority in heaven and on earth has been given to me. Therefore go and make disciples of all nations, baptizing them in the name of the Father and of the Son and of the Holy Spirit, and teaching them to obey everything I have commanded you. And surely I am with you always, to the very end of the age. (Matthew 28:18-20)

God's description of His mission-- to disciple all nations-- includes which two parts:

_____

_____

Can only pastors or professional ministers do all the jobs required to fulfill this mission?

_____

How many types of people, jobs, and ministries would be needed to teach people God's ways and to follow everything Jesus commanded?

_____

Why doesn't Jesus tell His disciples more specifically what to do, to fulfill the Great Commission?

_____

_____

Does the Great Commission sound as if you need to wait to be employed in it? Do you need to wait until God leads or reveals your particular destiny, or until you've fulfilled a timeline you created for your life?

_____

What could happen if you wait?

_____

Whatever your hand finds to do, do it with all your might. (Ecclesiastes 9:10)

Whatever you do, do it all for the glory of God. (1 Corinthians 10:31)

Do these verses make it sound as if there is just one valid job in the Kingdom?

_____

What two things are more important than the job you pick?

_____

_____

Consider the statement that "The problem you see is the problem you're called to fix." How is this Scriptural?

_____

_____

Whatever you do, work heartily as for the Lord and not for men. (Colossians 3:23).

Is your mission in life really about you?

_____

List a few ways that the world system trains you to think about men more than the Lord when you work.

_____

_____

_____

Does Scripture exhort you to spend lots of time trying to pinpoint your specific purpose or calling?

_____

_____

Will you miss God's best if you don't figure it all out early in life?

_____

He who loves his life will lose it; and he who hates his life in this world shall keep it to life eternal. (John 12:25)

What will happen if you love your own life?

_____

How should you handle your own pursuits and goals?

_____

_____

While the people were listening to this, Jesus proceeded to tell them a parable, because He was near Jerusalem and they thought the kingdom of God would appear imminently. So He said, "A man of noble birth went to a distant country to lay claim to his kingship and then return. Beforehand, he called ten of his servants and gave them ten minas. 'Conduct business with this until I return,' he said...

When he returned from procuring his kingship, he summoned the servants to whom he had given the money, to find out what each one had earned. The first servant came forward and said, 'Master, your mina has produced ten more minas.' His master replied, 'Well done, good servant! Because you have been faithful in a very small matter, you shall have authority over ten cities.' The second servant came and said, 'Master, your mina has made five minas. 'And to this one he said, 'You shall have authority over five cities.'

Then another servant came and said, 'Master, here is your mina, which I have laid away in a piece of cloth. For I was afraid of you, because you are a harsh man. You withdraw what you did not deposit and reap what you did not sow.' His master replied, 'You wicked servant, I will judge you by your own words. So you knew that I am a harsh man, withdrawing what I did not deposit and reaping what I did not sow? Why then did you not deposit my money in the bank, and upon my return I could have collected it with interest?'

Then he told those standing by, 'Take the mina from him and give it to the one who has ten minas.' 'Master,' they said, 'he already has ten!' He replied, 'I tell you that everyone who has will be given more; but the one who does not have, even what he has will be taken away from him..." (Luke 19:11-19)

What thought caused Jesus to tell the crowds this parable about investing their resources? What point about the Kingdom's timeline was He trying to make?

_____

_____

What did the master initially tell each servant, to whom He gave money?

_____

Did the master give each servant specific instructions about what to do?

_____

_____

Did the master control what the servants did, and when they did it?

_____

Does God control the activity or timing with which you do everything for Him? Who has authority over that?

_____

What was the main thing the master was hoping each servant would do?

_____

_____

Why did the servant who hid the money hide it?

_____

How does fear prevent people from fully investing themselves in God's Kingdom?

_____

_____

What reward did the master give for the servants' investment? What was he looking to give away?

_____

What will you be given as a reward for stewarding your own authority over yourself and your good decisions, when you invest in His Kingdom on earth?

_____

→ If you did not know that you will be rewarded for your risk and investment in growing God's kingdom, or if the idea of heavenly return does not motivate you, pray and ask the Lord why not. Consider journaling about it. Meditating on this truth is powerful.

DISCOVERING PURPOSE

When our enemies heard that we knew what they were going to do, and that God had frustrated their plan, we all returned to the wall, each to his work. From that day on, half of my servants worked on construction, and half held the spears, shields, bows, and coats of mail. And the leaders stood behind the whole house of Judah who were building on the wall... (Nehemiah 4:15-16)

Nehemiah was charged with rebuilding the walls of Jerusalem after the city had been torn down. Did everyone all have the same job?

_____

Think of rebuilding a wall like building God's Kingdom. Do Christians all have the same job in building God's Kingdom today?

_____

Think about the different people involved in bringing you to know Jesus. List some different roles they played.

_____

_____

_____

List some other ways you see Christians actively involved in society today.

_____

_____

_____

Nehemiah's wall would have been very large. How does everyone doing their piece help build and protect the city of God?

_____

_____

Those who carried burdens were loaded in such a way that each labored on the work with one hand and held his weapon with the other. And each of the builders had his sword strapped at his side while he built. (Nehemiah 4:17-18)

What were the two items each person stationed on the wall had with them as they worked?

_____

_____

What were the two components of their job? (What were the labor and the weapons for?)

_____

_____

Did it matter where each person on the wall was? Did their general job description differ?

_____

What were the two results of each person taking their place? (What did their labor and weapons accomplish?)

_____

_____

As it is, there are many parts, but one body. The eye cannot say to the hand, "I don't need you!" And the head cannot say to the feet, "I don't need you!" On the contrary, those parts of the body that seem to be weaker are indispensable, and the parts we think are less honorable are treated with special honor...

God has put the Body together, giving greater honor to the parts that lacked it so that there should be no division in the Body, but that its parts should have equal concern for each other. If one part suffers, every part suffers with it; if one part is honored, every part rejoices with it. Now you are the Body of Christ, and each one of you is a part of it. (1 Corinthians 12:20-27)

How many parts of your physical body are there? Which parts are not needed?

_____

_____

Who has put the Body of Christ, the Church, together?

_____

Are there parts of God's Kingdom that you are not interested in building? (Business, Politics, Education, Arts/Entertainment, etc...?) What would happen if Christians refused to enter one of these parts of society?

_____

_____

What happens when Christians enter them?

_____

_____

_____

How should we feel when a different group of Christians pursues something with excellence and results? Even if their cause doesn't resonate with us personally?

_____

_____

Have you seen Christians shooting themselves with "friendly fire"? In what ways?

_____

_____

_____

_____

Pray and ask God to reveal any area where you believe or behave in a way that is like "friendly fire."

_____

_____

_____

USING WHAT YOU HAVE: MOSES

Moses answered, "What if they [the Egyptians] do not believe me or listen to me and say, 'The Lord did not appear to you'?" Then the Lord said to him, "What is that in your hand?" "A staff," he replied. The Lord said, "Throw it on the ground…" Moses threw it on the ground and it became a snake, and he ran from it. Then the Lord said to him, "Reach out your hand and take it by the tail." So Moses reached out and took hold of the snake and it turned back into a staff in his hand. "This," said the Lord, "is so that they may believe that the Lord, the God of their fathers—the God of Abraham, the God of Isaac and the God of Jacob—has appeared to you."

Then the Lord said, "Put your hand inside your cloak." So Moses put his hand into his cloak, and when he took it out, the skin was leprous —it had become as white as snow. "Now put it back into your cloak," he said. So Moses put his hand back into his cloak, and when he took it out, it was restored, like the rest of his flesh.

Then the Lord said, "If they do not believe you or pay attention to the first sign, they may believe the second. But if they do not believe these two signs or listen to you, take some water from the Nile and pour it on the dry ground. The water you take from the river will become blood on the ground…" Moses said to the Lord, "Pardon your servant, Lord. I have never been eloquent, neither in the past nor since you have spoken to your servant. I am slow of speech and tongue." The Lord said to him, "Who gave human beings their mouths? Who makes them deaf or mute? Who gives them sight or makes them blind? Is it not I, the Lord? Now go; I will help you speak and will teach you what to say." (Exodus 4:1-13)

How did God respond to Moses' feelings that he was not qualified or able to fight?

_____

_____

_____

Moses was a shepherd with a simple staff in his hands. What did God use as his weapon?

_____

God used what Moses already had "in his hand" to defeat Egypt. What background, training, or personality traits do you already have "in your hand?"

_____

_____

_____

Have you rejected anything God has put in your hands as not fantastic enough to be used by Him?

_____

_____

Does God say you need to have special training, followers, or formidable equipment to make a difference for Him?

_____

Does God intend to back you up when you go out to fight? What can you rely on?

_____

_____

Does your mission have to fit your natural strengths?

_____

Does your mission have to fulfill everything you've ever dreamed of?

_____

After 400 years of enslavement under Pharaoh, God had a problem He needed fixing and Moses was swept into that. What problems does God have in this season that need fixing right around you?

_____

_____

_____

But Moses said, "Pardon your servant, Lord. Please send someone else. Then the Lord's anger burned against Moses and he said, "What about your brother, Aaron the Levite? I know he can speak well. He is already on his way to meet you, and he will be glad to see you. You shall speak to him and put words in his mouth; I will help both of you speak and will teach you what to do. He will speak to the people for you, and it will be as if he were your mouth and as if you were God to him. But take this staff in your hand so you can perform the signs with it." (Exodus 4:14-17).

Does God like it when He wants us to go for Him, but we won't?

_____

Does God see your limitations as His own limitations?

_____

Does God see your limitation as disqualifying you?

_____

Why doesn't having real limitations excuse you from fighting where He needs you?

_____

_____

Was God able to solve Moses' inadequacy problems? How?

_____

_____

Did God take away His approval, His mission, or His love from Moses just because Moses hesitated? Why not?

_____

_____

ACCEPTING YOUR PIECE: DAVID

God said to [King David], "You shall not build a house for My name because you are a man of war and have shed blood." Yet the Lord, the God of Israel, chose me from all the house of my father to be king over Israel forever. For He has chosen Judah to be a leader; and in the house of Judah, my father's house, and among the sons of my father He took pleasure in me to make me king over all Israel. (1 Chronicles 2:3-4)

David was not allowed to build God's Temple because he was a warrior and had killed people in battle. Yet he recorded how he was beloved by God anyway as the King of Judah. Did this bother David? Why not?

_____

_____

_____

Does God want you to wish you were someone else, with different talents or passions?

_____

_____

David and Joshua were both warriors. Joseph and Daniel were foreign advisers. Abraham and Moses met with God personally in the wilderness. Did God intend everyone to serve Him in the same ways? What does He understand about His mission?

_____

_____

REFLECTION QUESTION:

❖ What is God's greater mission on earth?
  → *Can I accept my unique place in it?*

WEEK 6: THE GREAT COMMISSION

Call to Action- Say "Yes" to Sharing Your Faith and Being a Witness

Main Points-

- "Lost" is a real condition with real eternal consequences.
- Jesus had great compassion for the lost, and we should too.
- He asks us to enter into His mission and accept it as our own.
- We must be unashamed about this.
- It takes courage to accept ourselves, but God has a place in the battle that fit us and is right near us.
- He needs many, many different kinds of warriors and witnesses. Everything can be used to bring more of Him into the earth.

Next Steps-

- ❖ *Write your testimony* of how you came to Christ. Pray for moments to share relevant pieces with those around you.
- ❖ *Think of several questions* you could ask people to get them talking about their beliefs with the goal of being able to share relevant truths or parts of your testimony with them.
- ❖ Find a few ways you can *reach out* beyond your church, i.e. through charity, service, evangelism, or discipleship opportunities in your local area.
- ❖ If possible, consider a *ministerial occupation* or a *ministerial component* of your job. Pray and ask God for direction or counsel on how He would like to show more of His character, love, and ways to the world through you in this season.

Key Scripture to Meditate on:

For I am not ashamed of the gospel, for it is the power of God for salvation to everyone who believes... (Romans 1:16)

www.ingramcontent.com/pod-product-compliance
Lightning Source LLC
Chambersburg PA
CBHW081631040426

42449CB00014B/3254